1.75

PRIVATE VIEW OF A PUBLIC MAN

Photo : *Navana Ltd.*

LEYTON RICHARDS IN 1938

[*frontispiece*

PRIVATE VIEW OF A PUBLIC MAN

The Life of Leyton Richards

BY

EDITH RYLEY RICHARDS

London
GEORGE ALLEN AND UNWIN LTD
RUSKIN HOUSE MUSEUM STREET

FIRST PUBLISHED IN 1950

PRINTED IN GREAT BRITAIN
in 11pt. Granjon type
BY HEADLEY BROTHERS
109 KINGSWAY, W.C.2
AND ASHFORD, KENT

To Our Children

MARGARET

JOYCE

CAROLA

Preface

A MAN'S WIFE is not, for many reasons, his best biographer. Yet, when various friends represented to me that Leyton Richards' life ought to be written, I was in a difficulty. He had lived and worked in many different spheres and only I had been in touch with him in more than one or two of them. I set about collecting the material for " some one " to use, became completely absorbed in it, and found that I wanted to use it myself.

Private and family relationships have only been touched upon as they affected his public life. To write a biography with them in the foreground would be to produce a companion volume of a different character. It might be called " A Public Man in Private Life " and the psychology of human relationship would be its main theme.

I have tried, in this Life, to present an honest picture. Mature love is not blind, though it often pretends to be, because its nature is to be protective. I have kept before me Boswell's ideal of what a biography ought to be : " I profess to write not his panegyric which must be all praise, but his Life ; which great and good as he was, must not be supposed to be entirely perfect. In every picture there should be shade as well as light."

I believed I knew my husband as well as one human being can know another, which is always incompletely. Yet, in reviewing the events of his life and arranging them in sequence, I have come to know him even better. I have seen, in some measure, why he was what he was, and I have become more fully conscious of the growth and development in him. A further deepening of our relationship, therefore, has come about through the writing of this biography and therein is my reward.

EDITH R. RICHARDS
Mortimer Common 1949

Acknowledgments

My thanks are due to :

Mrs. Ruth L. Pearson, my sister-in-law, for reading the MSS. and making many helpful comments ; Miss Janet N. Barker, for collecting recollections and impressions of the Melbourne ministry ; the Editor of the *Christian Century* of Chicago for permission to quote various articles ; L.H.H. for permission to quote from an article in the *Christian Century* ; the Editor of the *Christian World* for permission to quote articles by Martin Pew, and the Rev. F. C. Spurr and others ; the Editor of *The Spectator* for permission to quote from an article by Mr. Harold Nicolson ; Messrs. Cassell & Co. for permission to quote from Mr. Winston Churchill's, *The Gathering Storm* ; the Editor of *The Times* and the Bishop of Birmingham for permission to quote from a tribute by the latter ; Mr. Fenner Brockway for permission to use matter from his Labour Leader report of the Mansion House trial ; Messrs. James Clarke & Co. for permission to quote from *Ambrose Shepherd* by his son, Eric Shepherd ; Miss Margery Griffith for kindly reading the proofs.

Contents

Illustrations

Chapter I

EARLY YEARS

I NEVER SAW my parents-in-law, Charles and Jessica Richards, for both had died within two years of my first meeting Leyton Richards. I have often looked at the enlarged snapshot of his mother which always hung on the wall near his desk. It is a strong, beautiful face, grave in expression, with profoundly sad eyes which look straight out of the picture with an impression of absolute sincerity. It was taken soon after her husband's death and to him she had been devoted. I have no photograph of Mr. Richards and he remains to me a dim figure, while she stands out from the past strong and forceful. I never heard one word of criticism of either parent pass Leyton's lips and in any case the analysis of persons was never one of his pastimes. I always wanted to know what they were like and my impression has been built up from his answers to my leading questions, from their manifest influence on him, and from accounts of others who knew them. One of these describes his father, in middle life, as tall and stooping with a much-lined face and a lack of self-confidence, a little fussy about detail, but kind and good ; and his mother as " tall and upright, very dignified, every inch a lady, rather austere and frightening ". Another writes of her as " Upright and honest as the day ; I got to really like her and missed her good counsel when she died ". Everyone who knew the Richards family speaks with admiration of her. She held strong convictions on politics and race, on war and religion. She was a Liberal and a Nonconformist and a forceful defender of her faith. She did not, I gather, suffer fools gladly and was apt to make people feel fools who were not. Through almost all her married life she had a struggle against poverty but to " owe no man anything " at whatever cost to themselves, was the family tradition. What she missed from life, under the proud front with which she faced her world, is told in part by a gold brooch left in a box of trinkets when she died. She had bought it with her first earnings when, already well on in life, she went out as a school house-keeper, after Mr. Richards's death following a long and painful

1

illness.   In 1906, on the night of the Liberal victory in all divisions in Manchester, she was sitting in her chair, already ill from heart disease, when the news of the result was brought up to her room.   She heard it with joyful excitement, clapped her hands with expressions of jubilation, and died.   The immediate cause of death was undoubtedly a sense of the triumph of her own political cause.   It is my great loss that I never knew her except indirectly.

One effect of his early years was that Leyton Richards was always tender-hearted about poverty and had little use for the voluntary kind.   He felt that those who extolled it either had security somewhere in the background through wealthier relations or friends, or had never tasted the dull sordidness of the real thing with its tiresome petty economies and frustrations, and its necessary day-by-day obsession with the problem of how to make both ends meet.

I have seen the house in Sheffield where he was born on March 12th, 1879.   It stands in a short row of small, semi-detached middle-class houses, built of red brick now much smoke-begrimed, with a north aspect, and, in the road outside, a few stunted trees growing in its dirty grass verges.   Leyton, who could never get too much sunshine, and who seemed to increase in vitality and energy as the thermometer rose above 90°, hated the memory of that house.

His father, Mr. Charles Richards, was not a chartered accountant of the modern variety, but he was "trained in accountancy" and was employed in that capacity by a Sheffield cutlery firm.   He was the eldest of four sons and his father owned a clothing and outfitting shop in the Market Place, Sheffield.   On the death of his father, Charles bought out his brothers and took over the shop.   It did not prove an advantageous transaction partly, I surmise, because of his own temperament.   He was too tender-hearted for the business world, and also, perhaps, too meticulous about detail so that he could not always see the larger issues.   He found the same pleasure in accurate account-keeping that many to-day find in crossword puzzles and he always kept an eye on the state of his own balance sheet.   But he was not a keen competitor, or a shrewd buyer ; nor was he always firm, much less ruthless, in making hard-up customers pay their bills. His chief interests, indeed, lay outside his business, in the political and social and religious questions of the day.   He devoured the speeches of Mr. Gladstone rather than those of the chairman of the Haberdashers' Company ; he studied the findings of the Higher

2

Critics with more zest than reports of the Stock Exchange. His religious outlook was modern for his generation and Leyton was always proud of the fact that he had nothing to un-learn later owing to theological and Biblical obscurantism in his home.

When the Market Square business was taken over the Charles Richards family moved into the rooms over the shop and, as the shop assistants lived in too, Mrs. Richards kept house for them in addition to her own family. She seems to have been a thoroughly competent housekeeper who used her considerable brains to save labour and to provide adequately for her large household. At the same time she kept up her other interests as best she could, sharing her husband's, and in addition, keeping up her musical interest. She played the piano well, and early in his life Leyton had violin lessons, till poverty necessitated the sale of her instrument and the cutting out of his lessons. I always felt he had an undeveloped musical capacity. Many years later, at the age of forty-three, he had a course of piano lessons from the organist of Collins St. Church, Melbourne, but, though he practised diligently when he could find time, it was too late to make anything of it; fingers were stiff and more pressing engagements often pushed out lessons and practising.

Leyton was the middle one of three surviving sons (twins had died in infancy); the elder, Rivelin, later became a timber merchant, and the younger, Carl, a bridge engineer, first in Canada and later in the U.S.A., where he still practices in the Oregon State Highway Commission, and with whom Leyton always kept up frequent correspondence.

The first photograph of Leyton shows a somewhat sulky little boy in a check frock, with ringlets draped over his neck towards the camera—mother's pride, son's shame, they were to be cut off the same afternoon that the photograph was taken. Nearly thirty years later their owner, still shamefaced, thrust a box into my hands and hastily retreated, saying, "Here, look at 'em, and burn 'em." I looked, and saw a mass of curls still golden and shimmering; they had been found among his mother's treasures at her death. The head where they grew was always kept well clipped in later life for fear the smallest unwanted tendril might appear.

His earliest conscious recollection is of his mother reading the newspaper at the breakfast table and excitedly telling him to go and tell his father, through the bathroom door, that the Czar of Russia had been assassinated. Who a Czar might be and what had befallen him were a complete mystery to the messenger, but evidently something horrifying.

After a period of living over the shop the family moved once more, and, this time, to a pleasanter house near the Botanical Gardens and the boys were sent to school at Wesley College Kindergarten Department. In the meantime the shop was not doing well and my father-in-law saw a gradual decline in income with which to meet his growing expenses. Therefore, when an opportunity presented itself of going to the U.S.A., it was accepted. Mrs. Richards had a brother there who owned a small factory and he offered to take his brother-in-law into the business as accountant, and so at the age of nine Leyton Richards embarked on the first of his twenty-eight transatlantic crossings.

The days of grimy red bricks, overcast skies, and dirty green grass, and the down-town shop, were suddenly and miraculously behind them and all kinds of adventures and excitements lay ahead. The family sailed from Liverpool to New York, cabin class on the *Britannic*; after a few days in New York they went by train up the Hudson, and on to Niagara Falls. To the three boys, alert, eager, energetic, the whole journey must have been a Paradise. Never in after years would Leyton hear, patiently, one question as to the unsullied delight of transatlantic or trans-continental American travel. He, so sensitive to noises of every kind, was always lulled to peaceful sleep on an American sleeping car, whereas a duck quacking in the distance or the early morning cheep-cheep of a bird, would wake him, and the slightest creaking of a window would send him night-prowling through the house. He has been known to knock on the door of a sleepy guest with a request that something might be stuffed into a rattling window of which the guest himself was quite unconscious. But as he loved America and loved trains, no other sedative was needed than sweet content.

After Niagara there were still further delights, including a journey across Ontario, reaching Detroit by train-ferry and so on to their final destination, Grand Rapids, Michigan. There we can picture the wonder and the excitement, the sense of space and colour and freedom. To the boys it must have been a deliriously happy adventure. But the boys' climax was, to their parents, anticlimax, which filled them with dismay. During the time they had been in

4

LEYTON RICHARDS AS A SCHOOLBOY IN 1893

[facing page 4

transit the brother-in-law who was to have employed Mr. Richards
had died and the post to which he was going no longer existed. It
was only in retrospect that the sons began to understand what anxiety
and consternation must have fallen upon their parents at the end of
their journey. Somehow Mr. Richards managed to acquire a small
factory for making little brass fittings such as curtain rings, but it
was all new to him and a forlorn hope from the start.

Grand Rapids was a new, raw, undeveloped town ; the wooden
house which was rented for the family was roomy with rough ground
round it leading on to open woods. But it had few comforts or
even conveniences. Water had to be pumped, logs cut and carried.
It was hard work for all of them, which the boys at first found new
and exciting, but their daily tasks soon palled. It was hard on their
parents and Mrs. Richards was very home-sick ; there was an almost
complete lack in this town, with its future all before it, of cultural
and intellectual contacts.

The children went to the public school where the pupils represented a number of nationalities. Familiar school subjects took on a
fresh interest ; sums in dollars and cents, history taught from the
American standpoint, caused many surprises and sometimes indignant repudiation. Never again did Leyton see the land of his birth
or its history entirely from the British point of view. He had
learned to salute the Stars and Stripes as well as the Union Jack and,
maybe, his life-long interest in foreign politics and international
affairs goes back to the time when he learnt world history from a
teacher who spoke his own language with a difference.

There were the children of one negro family in the school and as
they seemed desirable playmates, and Mr. and Mrs. Richards believed
whole-heartedly in racial equality, their boys were encouraged to
bring them home. As a result Leyton and his two brothers were
sent to Coventry by the whole of the rest of the school ; no one would
speak to them or play with them. Writing about it years later
Leyton tells how :

> finally the head of the school, who was fortunately a wise and tactful
> woman, called upon my mother. I do not know what happened,
> for, during the interview we were sent to play around the wood-pile ;
> but I do know that the exchange of views was somewhat stormy and
> that thereafter those negro children never darkened our doors again,
> nor we theirs. To our inevitable question, " Why? " there was no

reply except a parental, " It is better not," but looking back, I understand.   It was and is a constantly recurring dilemma in more than one area of life ; should children be made to suffer for their parents' principles, or should other means be taken to inoculate those principles?   In our case, the latter course was taken and not without success.

Apart from this episode, to be young in Grand Rapids was, to Leyton, very heaven.   In the summer there were berry picking parties and picnics ; in the winter, tobogganing and snowballing, the building of huge bonfires and the roasting of unknown and delectable eatables.   Always there was space and a sense of freedom under skies that seemed higher and brighter than in our damper climate.

The Richards family were only about two years in Grand Rapids. Business difficulties, and Mrs. Richards's home-sickness, drove them back to England by the time Leyton was eleven years old.   Yet he always thought and spoke of himself as " educated in America ", and so in a profound sense he was, for to have lived there was an awakening and a highly stimulating experience.   Once the negro episode was over, the three English boys had been not only welcomed but sought after in the homes of their school fellows, and they had been introduced to new ways of living and thinking.   When they returned to England, Leyton had possibly dropped behind his contemporaries in book learning, but he had far outstripped them in breadth of outlook, in mental alertness and in intellectual curiosity.   He could never grow up insular and from this time the world began to be his parish and he developed a wanderlust which was to nag at him till the end of his life.

He brought back, too, the love of the U.S.A. which only deepened as the years passed and he made frequent subsequent visits.   He was as much at home there as in his own country.   An American friend wrote to me after his death : " His liking for America was of course one of his attractive features to us.   We find so many English do not like ' Americans ', but Leyton did like that vague abstraction, America—just as we like ' dear England '."

It would have been a satisfaction to him to have devoted some continuous years of his life to work in the U.S.A.   During the first World War an invitation of the right kind came to him to undertake a college chaplaincy.   He was ready to accept when the invitation was withdrawn.   America had just come into the war and by then he was a convinced and avowed pacifist.

Whether he would have enjoyed America as exuberantly had he become a permanent resident in a fixed post, as he did as a frequent visitor, I could never be quite sure.

Chapter II

HARD TIMES AND NEW OPPORTUNITIES

WHEN THE RICHARDS family came back to England, for some reason unknown to me, their home, for a year or two, was in Hornsey. There they lived in a row of small houses, facing an identical row on the other side. The children were sent to the nearest and not very good Board School where one redeeming feature was a master who made Scripture a fascinating subject. To go from Grand Rapids to Hornsey must have felt like a prison sentence to the three boys. There was little or no money for expeditions into the country or for sight-seeing in London. At times even their food was chosen for quantity rather than the quality required by fast-growing boys. From this time onwards Leyton always hated the thought of living and working in London or even in one of its further dormitories and said that only a strong sense of duty would induce him to do so. Fifty years later, riding on a bus through the suburbs of South London, he exclaimed with extreme distaste :

> How hateful it all is ! Even the open spaces are only gaps between these endless suburbs ; there's no community sense here and nobody can count for anything in his neighbourhood ; it's just an amorphous mass of people with nothing in common.

He had it in him to "count" and naturally enjoyed "counting" but it was not only that. Always he must have space, not inside the house where he never seemed troubled by small rooms, but almost every house we lived in was chosen for a spacious outlook. Once we looked out on an agricultural fair ground, once on to a public bowling green, another time on to a park, and once we had hedges and fences removed from back and front garden to give us a feeling of spaciousness.

Fortunately the prison sentence was not for long. An opening occurred in Reading for his father to combine tailoring and accountancy on a small scale. He did the accounts for little shops and businesses and often found them in a mess, with their owners barely paying their way, and with little with which to pay their accountant.

His own books were always meticulously accurate and his sons inherited their father's book-keeping habits. Leyton and I, later, lived on various salaries, the scale of which was by no means always an ascending one ; at each change a careful budget was drawn up and we took steps to live within it and to plan ahead. When, for example, our first child was a few months old an education policy was taken out which matured in time to pay her fees at Oxford. Much wealthier friends once remarked that they could not afford to send their daughters to college, to which Leyton promptly retorted, "And we can't afford not to," knowing that our children must some day be self-supporting.

In Reading the Richards lived still in a small, unattractive house but it was in a pleasant, quiet road close to Whiteknights Park and the boys were sent to Kendrick School, which was of the Grammar School type. They attended Trinity Congregational Church where at that time Dr. Ambrose Shepherd was the Minister. He was a strange, shy man, who found social contacts difficult, but Mr. and Mrs. Richards found both spiritual help and intellectual stimulus in his exegetical preaching and their sons sat at his feet for reasons of their own. Years later Leyton wrote about Dr. Shepherd after his death :

> He had not been long in Reading and was paying his first call upon a family who numbered among its members three boys and a fine tom-cat. He was awkward and so were we, but the cat saved the situation by jumping on to the table. Immediately the visitor made a pea-shooter from a newspaper at hand and began to bombard the cat with a shower of paper pellets ; the boys found immediate occupation in maintaining the supply of ammunition and feline profanity made conversation superfluous. From that day forward the Minister had three staunch friends in fair weather and foul and even the cat did not disdain his caresses . . . I remember how my brothers and I followed him round from meeting to meeting during his candidature for the Reading School Board, at each place somehow securing the front seat and at each place stimulating the vociferous applause which was never wanting.

To Leyton, in his early 'teens, Dr. Shepherd was a hero ; later they became intimate friends and the older and the younger man found their minds singularly in tune though their temperaments were very different. Some of the sentences from the Doctor's

biography, written by his son, might apply equally to my husband :
" He was quite content that his congregation should be dry-eyed if
he saw good reason for supposing that they were active minded."
" His pulpit was a sort of altar on which, week by week, he offered
up the gift of himself."

The influence of Dr. Shepherd on Leyton's subsequent career was
deep and permanent.

The Richards family found altogether happy associations in their
new Church. A group of young people formed themselves into a
small rambling club and open air country life again became possible,
with long walks and expeditions on Saturday afternoons. The
party possessed one bicycle between them which they rode in turn.
One of them recalls how soon Leyton emerged as their leader, planning the route and choosing the exact spot for the picnic tea. If
the party sometimes rebelled it was not unknown for their leader to
desert them and return to Reading alone. He remained a lover of
picnics to the end of his days, and when later they became family
outings he still led them and we used to call him Moses leading the
children of Israel to the Promised Land. At times the children
would decide to pick their own spot for the picnic meal but it was
always a mistake. Moses would hurry on to the scene and point
out that in ten minutes the sun would be shining into their eyes, or
that the wind was a little east of south and they would soon feel cold.
He was always, and often annoyingly, right.

Life flowed by more calmly and pleasantly in Reading till Leyton
reached the age of 15 when again that tiresome family balance sheet
necessitated his leaving school. He was much interested in natural
history and at that time it was his ambition to work in the
laboratories at Kew Gardens. He was therefore glad when he got
employment with Suttons the seed merchants, where he was set to
testing the fertility of seeds and various other jobs. At the same
time he attended evening classes in agriculture in the newly-formed
Agricultural Department of Reading College, as it then was. He
was one of the first students to get the Agricultural Diploma.

Inside Trinity Congregational Church he was finding an outlet in
another direction ; he was learning, through Sunday School work
and Christian Endeavour, to speak in public. The Church had
responsibility for several village chapels within a few miles of
Reading, having general oversight of them and supplying them with

lay preachers for the conduct of their Sunday services.   Leyton began
going out to these village " causes " with one of the deacons, driving
a horse and trap.   After a time he was allowed to read the lessons,
which he prepared then as always with great care.   There came a
Sunday when he was promoted to leading in prayer ; he was
extremely nervous and confessed he felt he would only be able to
utter a few sentences.   But as it turned out he couldn't stop ; words
flowed out of him ; he prayed with special fervour for " him who
was about to preach " ; at the end of twenty minutes a tug from
behind by this individual forced him to a closure.   From this and
later experience he was convinced that the so-called extemporare
prayer, characteristic of Free Church worship, should not be left to
the inspiration of the moment but should be carefully thought out
beforehand in the devotional privacy of a man's study.   He always
took trouble over every part of a service, looking up the lessons in
Authorized, Revised and one of the modern translations, choosing
beauty of language where possible but never sacrificing intelligibility
to it.   Nothing irritated him more in a service in any denomination
than obvious signs of slip-shod and hasty preparation.   As for the
flow of words, they came easily to him all his life in private.   In
public he disliked speaking without careful preparation.   No one,
I think, could accuse him of being *wordy* but he always had so much
to put into words.   In private he loved being listened to and took
some trouble to find audiences, which was never difficult ; he
particularly enjoyed arguments and provocative questions and comments.   In later life, when he had to prepare two sermons a week,
he used to say how much easier it would be if each could last
2½ hours, like a famous missionary one preached by John Angell
James in Carrs Lane Church, " How much more quickly I could
then prepare."   For it was pruning and condensing which took
the time and eliminating quite twice as much material as finally
appeared.   It was Dr. Shepherd's influence that set his feet early
on the path of solid expository preaching.   He first conducted a
whole service in a Presbyterian Church in Aston Tirrold, Berkshire.

Not only was he appearing in village pulpits at this stage but also
on Liberal Party platforms.   Those who heard him at that time
recall a youthful eloquence which was quite remarkable.   Once
when he was still little more than a schoolboy, at the end of a
political speech a voice from the hall shouted, " Not bad for a kid."

Like a flash the kid replied, " There's the highest authority for taking heed to what comes out of the mouths of babes and sucklings."

Several years passed : he was still at Suttons, and full of zest in his many activities, and he had reached his nineteenth birthday. One day Dr. Shepherd summoned him to his study and asked if he had ever considered offering himself for the ministry. Leyton confessed that he felt deeply called in that direction but that it was impossible for financial reasons. He was supporting himself and could not dream of becoming a charge to his parents. To enter the Congregational ministry would require three years of general University education followed by three years at a theological college. Dr. Shepherd, now knowing his young friend's mind, immediately set about raising the necessary funds. Several members of Trinity Congregational Church generously promised to see him through on a moderate but adequate allowance. It was a joyful opening of the way but there was a hard grind ahead. Leyton had left school four years before and had never, in any case, excelled in the learning of languages : he would now need Latin, already very rusty, and Greek, an entirely new subject. These must be produced for Glasgow University where he was to take his M.A. Later, at Mansfield College, Oxford, Hebrew would also be required. He needed special coaching, not to say cramming, before he could even tackle Glasgow University Entrance. Gordons College, Aberdeen, had special arrangements to meet such cases and to Aberdeen therefore he went for a preliminary year.

There he shared rooms with another man, who was, at the age of twenty-five, preparing to enter the ministry. A less promising combination of fellow lodgers could hardly be imagined. One was artistic, imaginative, erratic in the keeping of hours ; Leyton was logical, scientific in outlook, tidy and orderly to the last button and the last lecture notes, thrifty by necessity, and Puritan in his recreations and Spartan in his personal habits. But they had in common, poverty, high spirits, inquiring minds, quick tempers and ready tongues. Many were the battles of wit and words across the table they shared for meals and for study. Every few months they decided to part but always made it up again and the friendship begun in Aberdeen in 1899 was never broken.

Another friendship was formed in Aberdeen, which had an important bearing on the course of Leyton's later life ; it was with a

University student, Willie Wood by name, whose home was in Peterhead, forty miles farther north. The Wood family opened their hospitable doors to Leyton and through them, who were Congregationalists, he was introduced to their church and often found himself in its pulpit. In that most easterly Scottish town, known for its convict prison, its herring fishery and its red granite, the biting winds outside are forgotten in the warmth of the hospitality inside its solidly built houses.

The allowance which Leyton received from Reading friends, though covering University terms, left little margin for the five months long summer vacations of Scottish Universities. Preaching engagements, and an occasional article to a popular paper on such subjects as " Some Notable Things about Railways, by a Traveller ", or "Survivals—Why a Frock Coat has Buttons Behind ", were a small source of revenue but not enough and it was unthinkable to lay the burden of keeping him on his parents, so he turned his thoughts to the possibility of summer voyages on tramp steamers where at least he would have board and lodging and at the same time satisfy his craving to see the world. How his first voyage came about is best told in the words of Mr. Walter Watson who was partly responsible for making it possible : it must be explained that he always called my husband " Joe "—incidentally a name which seems to me to fit him better than his own.

It would be about May 1900 that Joe and I first met in Union Street, Aberdeen. It was a night never to be forgotten. Aberdeen was rejoicing over the fact that Baden-Powell had been relieved by our British Army in S. Africa. Bernard Ford, my chum, was 3rd Engineer of the *St. Bernard*, a steamer which was registered at West Hartlepool. My brother, James, was the Chief Engineer and I was the 2nd Engineer. The ship was in Aberdeen and had only got berthed when the good news came to the City. All business was suspended and everybody joined in the rejoicing. Bernard Ford and I went up to Union Street and we joined the students which ended up in Joe and his fellow students going with us on board for a feed and persuading the Chief Officer to get some rockets out and some signals of distress and we let them off and illuminated the harbour till 2 a.m. That was the start of many happy days together.

From that beginning Joe was signed on as 4th Engineer on the *St. Bernard* with his keep and nominal pay of 1s. a month.

They sailed from South Shields to Naples and from Italy they sailed to New York where Mr. Watson recalls :

> We had a good time in the City and attended the Church in Brooklyn. Dr. Hillis was the Preacher. After the morning service we were shown round the Church and Vestries. I remember sitting in the Pastor's chair, and got hold of Joe and sat him down. Little did we think then that later in life he would occupy the pulpit himself.

During other long vacations other voyages followed and Mr. Watson writes further :

> My brother, Captain Morgan and the Chief Officer were always ready for an argument with the three youngsters, either Politics, Religion or Navigation. When Joe came on board he really was a helper to Bernard and myself. The study of logic was one of our main talks and hour after hour I would lie in the bunk and Joe would get on the settee and we would argue and often knock for Bernard to come in and find another way out of the conflict. Next day we would tackle the other three and many a time I have missed an afternoon sleep, and not content Joe would bring a book down in the engine-room and sit thinking, then just say, "Walter, I got it now." That persistence won many a talk. Quiet, calm, and we would search all the books we could get hold of to get the truth. To-day I think of the happy evenings in the Southern Seas. Our portable organ was carried on deck and we had some jolly nights singing the old shanties and songs. And generally finished up with a reading and a prayer. Sunday was a great night. The ship's crew off duty used to come voluntary under the awning, and I usually used to give a talk. And we sang the old tunes, Joe joined us. And in the quiet of an evening hour on the lifeboat deck he told me of a greater desire there was, something deeper than logic. An urge to tell folk of a quieter and better life to be lived. We did not always agree but on fundamentals of life we did.

I have set this down at length, just as Mr. Watson wrote it to me, because I believe it shows that training for the Christian ministry is wider than the lecture room and the study. "Joe" had small Latin and less Greek but who can deny that on board the *St. Bernard* he was being prepared for his life work?

Chapter III

GLASGOW

IN THE AUTUMN of 1900 Leyton was ready to enter Glasgow University. By this time Dr. Ambrose Shepherd had moved from Reading to Elgin Place Congregational Church, Glasgow, so that the association between them developed and deepened still further. Leyton helped to run a Men's Sunday Afternoon Meeting at Elgin Place, and also helped the very absent-minded Doctor to remember his engagements, public and private, and he was treated almost as a member of the Shepherd family.

There was much to stimulate the new student, both in the classroom and in the various University societies. There were many distinguished men on the University staff, including Henry Jones and Adamson in Philosophy and Walter Raleigh in the English Department. Quickly Leyton became immersed in the Dialectic Society and in the University Liberal Club, in both of which he was associated with Dr. Ivy McKenzie who became a life-long friend. In his 2nd and 3rd years he became first, Secretary, and then, President of the two Societies. This brought him in touch with many distinguished men in the political and literary spheres who came as speakers. He kept letters from Winston Churchill, Rosebery, Asquith, Grey, Bernard Shaw and others, all surprisingly written with their own hands; apparently typewriters and dictation were not yet in common use by public men.

Leyton himself frequently spoke and debated in both Societies and Prof. Walter Raleigh said of him : " He is one of the very few natural orators I have heard." In his first term at a Union debate at which Haldane was the speaker, a University reporter wrote, " But *the* speech of the evening was that of Leyton Richards. He has not yet stopped the nonconformist preacher's mannerisms, but he made a powerful and eloquent speech." Later that year, in a debate against Edinburgh, it is recorded : " Mr. Richards had his facts at his finger tips as usual and set them forth with that force that causes consideration in the benches opposite." . . . " He is without doubt the best debater we have at College. His faults as a speaker are the use of too emphatic language, too many adjectives and a revel in superlatives. Time and practice will cure that."

Prof. Raleigh described him as " a natural orator " but behind the oratory was much hard work and burning of midnight oil. When Charles McCready was congratulated on his genius as an actor he replied, " Inspiration is all very well, but the painstaking labour of a man with a conscience is better." Leyton would have whole-heartedly endorsed that. No one outside his family knows the wearing and exacting labour which lay behind his public speaking. It was symbolic of his attitude that he considered that no man could do really good work in his slippers! He started each working day in outdoor shoes, always cleaned by himself, however busy he might be ; even during the many years when we had a thoroughly adequate resident domestic staff, he thought it unfitting that a man should allow a woman to clean his shoes.

When Leyton was secretary of the University Liberal Club in 1902, John Morley consented to stand for the Rectorial Chair against the Rt. Hon. George Wyndham put up by the Conservatives. Toryism was in the ascendancy in the country and the Jingoism which was the aftermath of the Boer War was rife in the University as elsewhere. It was therefore a hard fight, for John Morley was dubbed a " pro-Boer ". He had a staunch supporter and advocate in the young secretary of the Liberal Club who put all his energies into the struggle. One of his supporting speeches at this time was described from two points of view in the *Glasgow University Magazine*. A Conservative wrote :

> Mr. Spens was followed by Mr. L.R. who refrained from denouncing concentration camps and Mr. Chamberlain in order to show in what respects he differs from a pro-Boer. He has a particu-larly high opinion of our enemies, the Boers. Indeed, if he had his way of it, I have no doubt he would have selected Mr. Kruger as the candidate for Rectorial honours. As for his speech, it could not properly be termed a sermon for it had no text—at least none that could be found in the King's speech. When Mr. Richards turns curate I must hear him preach.

And a Liberal wrote :

> Then our Richards. The finest speech ever he made. He departed wholly from his usual style of smiting his opponents. He sternly

rebuked them for that slanderous epithet " pro-Boer ". It was the subterfuge of unscrupulous politicians, an appeal to the ignorant and unthinking, and a dishonest weapon to use against those who loved their country and honestly expressed what they thought was best for her. It was a grave instance of political immorality. The finest speech I ever heard in the Union.

If this wasn't his usual smiting what must other speeches have been?

There are many such references to Leyton in the *University Magazine* of his three Glasgow years. He worked with steady persistence at the required subjects for his M.A. degree but all his spare time was given to politics and debates. I look in vain for references to him in the reports of the Theological Society or the Student Christian Movement. In fact, two solemn young men, representing the latter, once waited upon him to ask him to resign from that Society on account of his too broad views and his capacity for spoiling the harmonious atmosphere of their meetings. I have only heard his side of the incident and I can well believe that the accusations were only too true, yet I cannot think of that brief encounter without amusement for I know what heart searchings there must have been in the S.C.M. before such a step was taken. But the culprit absolutely refused to be turned out, pleading Not Guilty to any moral delinquency which would have justified such expulsion. The two young men went sadly away with the problem of what to do with Leyton Richards still unsolved. He never really spoke the language then current in the S.C.M. so I doubt whether, in point of fact, he was often afterwards present to embarrass the members at their meetings.

He was frequently, in later years, to be accused of " taking politics into the pulpit ", but it could equally be said of him that he took religion into politics and on to the political platform. I have heard him turn a party election meeting into something indistinguishable from a religious meeting. He believed that ordinary men and women would respond to the very highest ideals and that politicians make a mistake in pitching their propaganda on the level of an appeal to self interest. Indeed, his ideal for his country was that it might become a theocracy and he always saw political issues, as did the Hebrew prophets, *sub specie aeternitatis*. As an example of this I quote a letter from a high school mistress written to me after his death :

We had had lessons, a lecture and a film on T.V.A. and it had seemed a clever plan but when Leyton Richards lectured on it to us we were lifted above the material plan to a vision of how much more it could be. I think it was the only time during those barren war years that I heard anyone give the girls sheer practical Christian idealism, and it was good to see their instant response.

From his earliest years to the very end he was deeply interested in politics, especially foreign politics, which he followed closely and continuously. He was urged many times to make Parliament his career and on more than one occasion he was offered the money which would have made it possible for him to stand.

One of his oldest friends wrote to me forty years later that he had always regretted Leyton's choice of the Church for his life work, that he would have served his day and generation to greater effect if he had taken his idealism and his gifts into Parliament where he would have gone far. Others, both inside and outside the Church, have expressed much the same opinion. But Leyton himself never seriously wavered in the choice he had made. To " preach Jesus Christ " seemed to him the best contribution he could make to his country's political life, for he believed that only citizens steeped in the knowledge of Christianity and prepared to accept its demands would make our politics, home and foreign, Christian. Neither did he ever lose faith that such a standard is attainable and that a grave responsibility rests on the Church for its attainment. And, incidentally, he considered that a man's attitude to his income tax was a kind of touchstone by which his religious values could be judged— whether he tried to dodge paying any of it and whether he grudged paying any part of it which went towards public services he professed to believe in.

The Glasgow years had been full of zest and high spirits, serious pursuits and light-hearted recreations. His last term was clouded by the onset of his father's last, long drawn out and painful illness, necessitating one or two emergency visits to his Reading home to lend a hand.

The final entry about him in the *Glasgow University Magazine* reads :

Mr. Richards, whose photograph appears in our pages, needs no introduction. It may comfort him in his Oxford exile to reflect that for many a day the echoes of his eloquence will ring in our ears.

Chapter IV

OXFORD

AT FIRST OXFORD did indeed feel like exile ; there were so many more rules and regulations there, certain dinners which had to be eaten in Hall instead of a pair of kippers supported by scones and oatcakes in simple, sometimes sordid, lodgings in Glasgow. There was more oversight and less freedom and self-determination. Leyton found, too, that his flow of talk and his boisterous high spirits were not universally appreciated and that his enthusiasms were considered by some too enthusiastic. And he became more than ever conscious of the gaps in his early education : he knew a good deal about many things but his fellow students at Mansfield, mostly Oxford and Cambridge graduates, knew a great deal about a few things. And his poverty cut him out of some of the recreations which were commonplaces to most of his associates. Tennis clothes and a tennis racket were beyond his purse. On the Clyde he had managed a boat very pleasantly in his second-best every-day suit ; the Isis seemed to demand white flannels and a blazer. So he was, I imagine, though he never confessed it, rather a lonely young man during his first term or two in Oxford. But he was never one given to self-pity or introspection and he couldn't possibly feel lonely long, for he found good comrades in the other eight men of his " year " at Mansfield. Two of them especially became intimate friends—Sidney M. Berry and my brother, William Winstanley Pearson, commonly called Willie. It was considered a particularly able Mansfield year, the others being C. B. Young, R. K. Evans, W. H. Coats, Eric Roberts, Herbert Morgan, and J. A. Hadfield.

The staff was distinguished for its weighty scholarship, which laid the foundation for Mansfield's full acceptance in the life of the University where, in my father's youth, Nonconformists had not even been admitted. Dr. Fairbairn was Principal, surrounded by a galaxy of scholars—Dr. Buchanan Gray for Old Testament, Dr. Soutar for New Testament, Dr. Vernon Bartlett for Church History, Mr. Thatcher for Hebrew. An important addition to these was

Frank Lenwood, not only New Testament tutor inside Mansfield, but the first to hold the position of Pastor to the Nonconformists in the University, where he had deep and widespread influence.

Mansfield College Chapel and its Sunday services held a high and honoured place in the religious life of Oxford, and drew large congregations.

Dr. Fairbairn had, I fancy, a specially soft spot for Leyton Richards, this duck-out-of-water student from far north. However that may be, he was uniformly kind to him and seemed to take special interest in his doings and in his development.

At the time of the Doctor's death my husband wrote of him :

"The Doctor" has gone beyond mortal ken. There is only one "Doctor" to a Mansfield man, and he was both the scholar and the friend. We loved "the Doctor" and I believe he loved us ; at any rate, he made us feel that he did, and the collegiate life of Mansfield, in consequence, had all the close camaraderie of family feeling. "The Doctor" was our "Father in God", not by reason of holy orders or grace bestowed in priestly functionings (such things he abhorred with all the vigour of his rugged Puritanism) but by reason of that genial—albeit to the freshman somewhat awesome—paternal benevolence that radiated from him. He was one of the Olympians, and the rôle befitted him—it clung to him as part of himself, and he never tried to cast it off by condescension in personal intercourse. That was why to know "the Doctor" was such a bracing experience ; he met you, not on your level, but on his, and in trying to climb to that height you breathed, for a time, the tonic air in which he throve and fought.

It was said of Dean Stanley that people used to go to the Abbey simply to hear him read the Lord's Prayer, and the same may be said of Dr. Fairbairn's benedictions. Often I have seen him sitting in his stall in the college chapel, the preacher for the day meanwhile making the fatal mistake of delivering an academic discourse to an academic congregation. Heads nodded, minds wandered, we longed for escape but then of a sudden we were on our feet for the benediction. "May grace, mercy and peace from God the Father, and His Son, Jesus Christ, be with you all, evermore." That was all, but we went out with the Doctor's blessing upon us, refreshed in soul.

There was one phrase continually upon his lips in prayer, and often in his lectures, and the phrase was an unconscious piece of self-description. Higher praise of the Father he could not frame than to call Him "gracious and kindly", and it was also his highest praise of man. "Gracious and kindly!" We sometimes smiled at the oft repetition of the phrase, but we had a deep affection for the man who repeated it: it came from his heart; it was himself and we knew it. . . .

The other member of the staff to whom Leyton turned with special appreciation and affection was Dr. Vernon Bartlett. One of my husband's gifts was the power of mimicry and never did a college staff offer such golden opportunities: each had his marked idiosyncrasies and mannerisms. In the same period W. H. Coats was a first-class caricaturist and at the end of each term, during the College concert on the last night, the caricatures of the session were displayed and an impersonation of each member of the staff was given by Leyton to the delight of everybody, sometimes including the wives of the caricatured, secreted behind a screen in case they might cramp his style.

The learning of Hebrew was a sore trial to Leyton and to some others. When Dr. Buchanan Gray had spent a whole term in taking his class through one short Psalm in the original, with meticulous, scholarly accuracy, a mild rebellion broke out, which left the staff unmoved. Thereupon Leyton and my brother Willie invented a labour-saving device known as the Hebrew Syndicate for the use of the linguistically weaker brethren. It pooled resources and minimized effort in the Hebrew work which had to be got through, and was a source of pride and satisfaction to its inventors whatever it may have been to their tutor and professor.

Sidney Berry and Leyton, among the students, were in considerable demand for preaching engagements up and down the country. Many Fridays, during term, a leather hat-box with its original surface quite worn away, was posted in Oxford: it contained Leyton's top hat, then the accepted Sunday head-gear for ministers and deacons at least. Its owner followed next day, in a cloth cap and every-day suit with his frock coat packed tightly in a small, well-worn leather Gladstone bag. He never felt at home in anything approaching finery and his best friend could not have said that a top hat became him.

There were no lectures at Mansfield on Monday morning as staff and students were expected to be away over the week-end preaching elsewhere. The College had several village chapels under its charge and was wholly responsible for supplying their pulpits.

During his second and third years in Oxford, first Leyton's father, then his mother died, both in the home of his eldest brother. Mr. Richards had been increasingly ill for several years. He struggled to carry on his business till it was no longer possible even to the most courageous. Leyton went home for a few hours whenever he could to help with the book-keeping, on which the slender family income depended.

When at last Mr. Richards's suffering was ended, Mrs. Richards wore no mourning and in 1905 that took some courage as it was most unusual and apt to be misinterpreted. As soon as she was able she turned out to earn her living, first as housekeeper to Walthamstow Hall, a girls' boarding school for the daughters of missionaries, and then, when that proved beyond her strength, as companion to an old lady. But she was already worn out and soon had to give in, and go back to her eldest son and his wife, Rivelin and Clara Richards, who did unselfish, willing service to both the parents in their last days.

In 1906, during his vacation, Leyton was speaking at a Liberal election meeting in Scotland when a telegram was handed to him on the platform, summoning him home to his mother. He travelled all night and arrived in time to have a few hours with her before, late on Saturday night, she died, in circumstances to which reference has already been made. It was characteristic of him that he fulfilled a preaching engagement in Reading on the following morning, rather than let the Church down.

These two bereavements, which clouded his College days, drew him very near to his friends Sidney Berry and Willie Pearson, for whose sympathetic understanding he never ceased to be grateful.

Chapter V

TWO PATHS MEET

I HAD GONE up to Somerville College in 1903, at the age of nineteen, to read for the English Honours School. Though I was three years younger than my brother Willie, as he had already taken a Cambridge degree before going to Mansfield, our time in Oxford synchronized. He was preparing himself for educational work in India under the London Missionary Society and though he had a few years in Calcutta under their auspices, he finally ended up on the staff of Rabindranath Tagore's school and became a collaborator with Mahatma Gandhi and C. F. Andrews in defending the rights of Indians in South Africa and Fiji, and, in general, forwarding Indian national aspirations.

One Sunday evening in the autumn of our third year he and I were sitting in deep arm-chairs by a large fire, reading, when there was a sudden sound of a rushing, leaping step on the stair and a tall, fair, ruddy, eager-faced, laughing young man burst into the room and into my life. He stood stock-still when he saw me and stared as if I had been Medusa herself. Rules of chaperonage were strict in Oxford forty-two years ago and a man and woman student were not allowed to meet, inside a house, except by special permission from their college authorities and then only in the presence of an older woman, or a married one of any age. (Young brides were in great demand as chaperones.) My brother, ever an easer of situations, with a flicker of amusement said : " Richards, this is my sister ; I am sure it will be all right for you to come in for a few minutes." In he came, but once his tongue was unloosed minutes were of no use to him, as all his friends well know and an hour or two passed before he remembered to go. He was full of the adventures of his day which had been spent in taking services in a village chapel. Always, as I was to learn later, a preaching engagement away from home took on the features of an adventure story with descriptions of his week-end host, or the deacons, or the performances of the choir, or the nature of the church secretary's notices: truth lost nothing in the telling and it was all told with light and life. Before the evening was over I knew quite a lot about him and he had learnt one or two things about me.

We did not meet again for some months but a few letters passed between us, his *billets-doux* usually taking the form of newspaper cuttings about something he thought would be of interest. As a friend of Willie's he had stayed in my home and preached for my father, who was also a minister, but each time in my absence. My parents, especially my mother, liked him. The following Easter he was having a week's holiday in Paris with Sidney Berry when my brother, to whom he had disclosed his state of mind, let him know of an unexpected preaching engagement in Manchester and an invitation to stay with my people. A chagrined Sidney Berry was left deserted in Paris and, as it turned out, a chagrined Leyton Richards arrived in Manchester to find that I was away staying with friends over the week-end. He managed still to be there on my return when I seriously lost caste with him. My journey had been a little complicated and when he asked by what railway lines I had travelled, I could not tell him. "But," he said, "what was the colour of the engine?" I just shook my head helplessly and he returned to the charge with: "Well, you *must* know the colour of the carriages?" Still I shook my head. He looked at me with a mixture of incredulity and pity. He was too transparent ever to disguise his surprise at ignorance, often to the discomforture of the ignorant.

During the summer term we met in Oxford twice, and on the third occasion, during our last week up, he proposed and was accepted. I am not one who sees things, as he did, in clear colours, yet the three or four momentous decisions of my life have been made with swift certainty and with the passage of time they have still seemed right.

Before he proposed Leyton's Mansfield training was complete and I had finished all the written work of my Finals, but had still to face the viva voce part of the examination. As it turned out at the very hour when I was appearing before my five examiners Leyton was putting his credentials to my father in Manchester.

The result was that more than half my mind was in the library at home where I knew that a pink, embarrassed young man was facing a much more formidable *viva* than I was. So absent-minded was I that I found myself asking a question of one of my examiners about some literary point as though we were engaged in pleasant, friendly conversation. As it happened, fortunately, to be Professor Raleigh he only smiled and said, " On this occasion I am supposed to be questioning *you*." Later, on hearing of our engagement, he sent me a charming letter. He had often heard Leyton speak on political platforms but, he wrote, " This election makes all the rest look foolish."

A biographer usually describes the wife of his subject, and at this distance of time I believe I could give a fairly objective, as well as subjective account of myself as I was at the age of twenty-two. But it would come ill from me and I must let facts themselves, and other people's opinions, speak for me.

My father, Samuel Pearson, was a Congregational minister and was successively in charge of churches in Steel House Lane, Birmingham, Great George Street Chapel, Liverpool, Highbury Quadrant, London, and finally at Broughton Park, Manchester, where he had been since I was five years of age. My mother, whose maiden name was Crosfield, came of an old Quaker family with many branches. Her parents, William and Eliza Crosfield, had, after much painful heart searching, left the Society of Friends to become Congregationalists, because of what they felt to be its lack of evangelical conviction and witness but they never ceased to feel deep attachment to the faith of their forefathers and a pride in their ancestry.

I had five brothers older than myself and one younger, and a sister, Dorothy, my constant friend and companion, two years my junior. My parents were both tall and so were all of us and my father used to say that he had thirty-six feet of sons.

At the age of fifteen, when Leyton was leaving school, I put my foot across a school threshold for the first time. Up till then, Dorothy and I had lessons from nine to twelve each morning in the nursery at the top of the house, from my father's youngest sister, Aunt Mary. In the afternoons we learnt music, French and drawing from three other ladies and sometimes played tennis and cricket with our brothers. The music mistress, Miss Warren, was an old lady with white hair dyed brown, who always wore a black bonnet and a beaded mantle. She was the daughter of Samuel Warren, the author of the first English detective novel. She gave me weighty performances of the Beethoven sonatas she was teaching me. Our education was entirely without pressure and I have no recollection of doing much work after tea except piano practising.

As I was approaching fifteen, my parents began to inquire about a number of boarding schools and the final choice lay between the Quaker school, The Mount, York, and St. Leonards in Scotland. My mother was Quakerly in her outlook and in her demeanour, but the balance was tipped in favour of St. Leonards by its more bracing climate and its country surroundings on the edge of the cliffs at St. Andrews. My parents believed, too, that it would be bracing in other ways. Up to this point I had been surrounded by Nonconformist and chiefly Congregational influences. Our French governess was chosen, not only for her accent, but for her Protestantism. Our nurses were chosen from Congregational backgrounds with one aberration—a French woman was engaged to improve our powers of French conversation. She was pretty and fascinating but, unfortunately, it was discovered that she flirted with a policeman when she took us for walks, so her reign, so highly entertaining to her young charges, was cut short after only a few weeks. We always attended Free Church services at home and on our summer holidays, which were long, for my father's churches gave him six free weeks a year. Now that I was in my teens it was considered that there should be a widening of contacts and experience and to St. Leonards therefore I was sent, where Episcopalianism and Presbytarianism were predominant. In September 1899, with many pangs at parting and yet with zest in the adventure, I joined a railway carriage full of girls all bound for my new school. Though, or perhaps because, I came from an exceptionally happy and harmonious home I took to boarding school like a duck to water and suffered no serious homesickness. Life did indeed open out and it was both physically and mentally bracing. One incident will illustrate the physical hardiness which was expected of us. I was summoned to the top of the table one wintry Sunday morning by my housemistress, Miss Sanders, who asked why my window had been shut when she returned from Early Service. I told her that there had been a coating of ice on my bath water—each of us had a cold hip-bath in our cubicles each morning. " You *muff* ! " was her withering comment.

And the emotional self-control and reserve demanded of us may be illustrated by another incident. On the first Sunday evening of each term, in our house, during a half-hour's hymn singing, we always began with a Hymn for Absent Friends which got more heart-rending as it went on. It began :

> Holy Father in Thy Mercy,
> Hear our anxious prayer,
> Keep our loved ones now far absent,
> 'Neath Thy care.

There was a girl who, each term, by the time the third verse came, was quietly sobbing and sniffling into her handkerchief. On one occasion a hand went up, the piano stopped playing and Miss Sanders's voice fell on the deathly silence, with : " Emily, we shall continue to sing this hymn till you learn to control yourself." We continued, and Emily learnt. And yet our housemistress was herself highly emotional, artistic, humorous, and exciting to live with.

The teaching in the main school was stimulating and interesting and I still remember the outline of my first lesson, on my first morning, which was an English one. The staff were given much freedom in their presentation of their subjects and they used it to advantage. There was no cramming or pressure, though I must confess I spent one long hot summer afternoon " kept in " with Margaret Thomas, now Lady Rhondda, to learn our Latin gender rhymes. Scripture was well taught : the first Isaiah came to life in the classroom and we spent a whole term getting an insight into the meaning behind the words—OLD and NEW Testaments. In the large school hall we listened enthralled, one Sunday afternoon, to the book of Esther read to us by the senior Scripture mistress. On another occasion Miss Lumsden held us by a recital of old Scottish Ballads.

There was much acting in the whole school, but I think our house excelled. Beatrice Forbes-Robertson was one of Miss Sanders's old girls and Irene and Violet Vanburgh were friends of hers and visited her. There was a tower to the house and it was occupied by Miss Freda Hawtrey, a relation of the celebrated actor, Charles Hawtrey : as a producer she was little short of a genius. With a caste entirely made up of schoolgirls she produced a moving performance of Sophocles's " Antigone ", to which the translator and various other Edinburgh people came. It was repeated several times and the girl who took the part of Creon threw herself so completely into it and so lived in it that she was obliged to have some weeks at home to recover ! To those who saw her acting it will always remain a grateful memory.

Our headmistress, Miss Grant, was a shy, reserved, unmistakably devout Christian woman, who so seldom spoke of religion that she made a deep impression when she did. During the latter part of my time at school she used a Sabbatical year to go to Egypt and India and on her return took a class in Comparative Religion with the VIth form which opened out new fields to our awakening minds.

Just before I left school Miss Sanders slightly shocked my parents by writing, " Edith is so delightfully cynical." Leyton never delighted in cynicism, least of all in mine ; he took it at its face value which the cynic seldom intends, for it is, in fact, mostly protective colouring. He used to look like a hurt child if I made a cynical remark, so I learnt to curb this tendency in me for his sake.

Another remark I must record was also a written one. A fellow student of his at Mansfield wrote to mutual friends of theirs in America. " Richards has become engaged to a very conventional girl ", which, in the indiscreet way people have, they repeated to me when they got to know me for themselves. I was, I suppose, inclined to be rather " proper ". I was certainly, by habit, law-abiding, having met so few laws either at home, at school, or at college, by which it was not easy to abide. " Delightfully cynical " and " very conventional " did not sound promising for the wife of Leyton Richards, nor my training in the matter of frozen bath water, as a life partner to one who preferred a room temperature of 65° to 70°. But I had certain assets, not of my making ; one was my relationship to six brothers who had pulled my long pig-tails, and chased me round the nursery table and burnt a pet stuffed elephant of mine at a Red Indian feast, as well as being the good comrades they always were to the two they called " the little girls " till my sister and I had long been grown up. The other and greatest asset was my parentage ; there was wisdom and tolerance, salted with humour in both my father and my mother, and their own perfect companionship gave their family the best of all inheritances.

This outline of my home background and early years brings me to the point where my path and Leyton Richards's converge. The important and fundamental things in our upbringing we had in common : more superficial things had been very different. Material privileges and opportunities had been mine which had not been his, but he had made more creative and original use of those which he had. To give only one example : I had been to Europe five times before I met him.   My first trip abroad was with my parents, to Italy and Paris, in the spring before I entered St. Leonards ; my father was a true art lover and it was an education to visit the galleries of France and Italy in his company.   My sister and three of my brothers inherited his artistic discrimination.   My mother, who had been a pupil of Collinwood's, did pleasant sketches in particularly pure, clean water-colour.   The events in our home life included my father's discovering of young and promising artists and in the buying of their pictures.   Francis Dodd painted portraits of three members of the family while still in his early twenties, and I believe that the first exhibition in England of Muirhead Bone's etchings was in the rooms of one of my brothers at Emmanuel College, Cambridge.

Leyton's upbringing on the other hand had not included much attention to the Arts.   I never willingly went to an Art Gallery in his company!   His opinions of the pictures were dogmatically expressed, but if he said, " That is the best picture on that wall," it often seemed to me to be the worst.

On family holidays abroad, in my youth, we always stayed in hotels or pensions where nearly all our fellow guests were English. We enjoyed the scenery of the countries we visited and, as five of us packed paint boxes, we brought back innumerable water-colour sketches good and bad, also lists of flowers, and botanical specimens. We visited Art Galleries and churches and historic buildings.   My mother spoke French and German and a little Italian, but was far too shy and retiring to make vocal use of them.   My father, whose knowledge of *modern* languages was scanty and his accent appalling, used to plunge in when necessary and amused both the family and the foreigner.   We carried a bit of home and of England with us wherever we went.

In contrast, Leyton, with even less aptitude for languages, in whatever country he travelled, took pains to get in touch with its people and its life.   I was to learn how stimulating, if sometimes physically exhausting, it was to travel with him, for he was continually alert to see, to learn and to understand.   On railway journeys he would talk to the people with gestures and with a modicum of execrable French or German ;   he would watch the passing landscape to observe the agricultural methods, the road construction, the building materials, the use of waterways, the gardens and orchards and the human figures visible.   He did all he could to scent the political atmosphere and to discover social conditions. He seemed to me to acquire more knowledge of a country in a month than most travellers do in years. He always tried to stay where he would meet only the people of the country.

My family had given their attention chiefly to the universal values of natural beauty and of art. Leyton appreciated natural beauty also and had more scientific knowledge of its details. To this he added an eager interest in discovering, as far as he could, the ethos of the country visited ; always, therefore, he came home with a more international outlook than he took with him, having tried to enter into ways of thinking and living other than our own.

In Oxford, then, in 1906, our two paths, which had begun so far apart, converged. We had much to give to each other and our union was to bring its own rich rewards, but the winning of the garland was not wholly "without dust and heat".

Because our engagement had been preceded by so few and such brief encounters and the courtship had been a lightning one, friends and relations, with the exception of my parents, were taken completely by surprise. Indeed, Mrs. Buchanan Gray, a friend of both of us, formally introduced us to each other outside Mansfield College Chapel the morning after we became engaged!

There were no future parents-in-law for me to be introduced to but the reactions in my own family were recorded in various letters at that time. My father's eldest sister, Aunt Louie (a second mother to us), wrote to another sister, Aunt Amy, "You will probably have heard by now the exciting news of Edith's engagement to Mr. Leyton Richards. It stirs us all very much, that is if one is not stunned. Dorothy returned from Edinburgh this afternoon and was knocked down on the doorstep by the news." And Aunt Mary writes : "Mr. Richards is a very strong personality, a great tall man, over six feet, with stubbly fair hair and a ruddy complexion. He talks like a torrent and is considered a very clever man by his Mansfield companions." A more romantic Aunt on the Crosfield side of the family described him as "a golden-haired Viking". My father wrote to Dr. Fairbairn that he was finding him over-boisterous, to which the Doctor replied that time and responsibility would soon cure that. He was to prove right: boisterousness gradually mellowed into a cheerful buoyancy.

Chapter VI

PETERHEAD

I HAVE ALREADY spoken of Leyton's association with Peterhead during his time in Aberdeen. All through his six years in Glasgow and Oxford he had returned there to preach from time to time, and his visits became frequent after the Congregational Church lost its minister in 1903. For two years the Church made diligent search for a successor, but could not find any who appealed to them. At last, in 1905, Mr. William Murray, the Church Secretary, addressed a letter to Leyton in Oxford, inviting him to become their minister, even though it would be fifteen months before he had completed his training and already the pastorate had been vacant for two years. Many of his friends and associates, though not his College Principal, felt he would be making a mistake "to bury himself in a small, remote Scottish town " so far from what they felt to be the " centre ". Even from the north of England it took more than a day to reach Peterhead. But Leyton himself judged differently. Already more than one large English Church was taking significant notice of him, but a " large sphere ", and what the world counts important, never carried weight with him : he seemed unconscious of such values. For himself, he put the preaching function of the ministry in the first place, before the organizing of church activities, or general, as opposed to specially needed, pastoral visitation. He knew that in this he would have the Peterhead congregation with him. He believed that they could take the best he had to give ; that solid thinking in the study and the pulpit would be met by solid thinking in the pew ; that what he preached would be digested before it was accepted ; that if it were rejected he would be told the reason why, man to man, and face to face. He therefore accepted the invitation and it proved a happy decision. Dr. Fairbairn was wont to say that a church could not have full use of both the head and the heels of a man : all the churches Leyton served had most use of his upper end, but none chose that it should be so with more open-eyed deliberation than his first, and his last.

His ordination took place on June 27th, 1906, and it followed the simple but solemn and dignified procedure of Congregationalism on such an occasion. It began with a statement in his own words of his religious and theological beliefs which included his conception of the nature of the Church :

> I hold that wherever there is a community of Christian believers, linked together in common worship and in common service, there is a Church. The qualification for membership of such a Church to me does not lie in forms and ceremonies, or in subscription to a written creed, or in allegiance to any human power, be he king, or priest, or presbyter, but only in character, grounded and built in Jesus Christ. The organization of local Churches into a centralized system, whether Presbyterian or Episcopal, is largely a matter of detail to be governed by the exigencies of the day and the demands of common life. But personally I value, above all the undoubted benefits of organization, the freedom which is given under Congregationalism to thought and action, and to the development of personality.

After the acceptance of the statement by the Church and the prayer of dedication, Dr. Fairbairn followed with the charge to the minister. After saying that " for years Mr. Richards and he had known each other, and the knowledge had been as gracious as the knowledge of any human being could be to another ", he went on :

> Mr. Richards is now a minister and he knows what a minister means. It is the opposite of a magister. . . . A magister is a great man who teaches, who commands, and directs the souls of men. A minister is a little man, who is ready to do anything to help men to better themselves.

Dr. Shepherd followed with a Charge to the Church which included the following sentences :

> They had invited their young friend to take his place in the ranks of the Christian ministry. The true preacher was essentially of the priestly spirit just in the degree that he possessed the heart of Christ, the high priest of humanity. . . . It was a priesthood in which we were all called to share, each to offer himself a living sacrifice to God and do what he could to bring others close to Him by whatever ministry seemed most available for that end. This was not to say that there were not functions associated with the priesthood of believers for the efficient discharge of which men with the requisite gifts and graces should be trained and set apart, but neither gifts nor training could make a man a priest or a minister. The only thing

that could make a man a New Testament minister was the priesthood of character, the presence of the Spirit and the power of eternal life. Every believer was called to this ministry, but not to the same distinctive place in it. . . .

There were people who appeared to think that the preacher had but to open his lips and his mouth would utter forth a sensible and effective discourse. Sermons that were sermons were not to be had on those terms, and a strong pulpit meant a stern study.

The high hopes of him, and the exacting ideals put before him that day left Leyton humbled and awed so that, he confessed, he would have felt inclined to run away were it not for his faith in the Gospel he felt called to preach and his deep conviction of man's need of it.

He was soon installed in the solid, red granite, three-storied Manse on Queen Street, the free use of which, together with £180 a year, made up his salary. It had been decided that we should not be married for about a year, during which time I was to have some instruction in cooking at the Manchester School of Domestic Economy. In the meanwhile Leyton's younger brother, Carl, who was working for engineering qualifications, lived with him. A housekeeper, Mrs. Moir, looked after them both, and so good and constantly recurring were her scones and oatcakes that even lean Leyton began to put on weight.

Peterhead is the most easterly point of Scotland and none but its solid granite houses would stand against its gales. The wind is salty and, during the months of fishing, it is seasoned also by the smoke of kippering : both the salt and the seasoning seem to match the local character.

The town had, at that time, a population of 15,000, with a considerable proportion of fisher folk engaged in the catching, curing and smoking of herring which the men followed round the coast. They were, therefore, only at home part of the year when the shoals were off the Buchan coast. Other occupations were granite quarrying, a woollen mill, and all the work connected with the large convict prison on the outskirts of the town. The steam-roller of urban life had not smoothed out the individuality, nor the idiosyncrasies of the inhabitants.

The typical Peterhead fisherman (or woman for that matter) allowed no one to do his thinking for him : his views on matters small and great were pithily expressed in broad Buchan which Leyton could admirably reproduce. There was no beating about the bush, as when Jeanie coming in late to a morning service and finding her regular seat occupied said audibly : " Coom oot o' that." Or there was Jamesie, a staunch upholder of " free prayer ", who waylaid the Episcopal minister, coming from the conduct of a service in the old people's institution, with, " I didna like yon prayers." When told that nevertheless they were the prayers of great saints, he retorted, " Aye, aye, maybe, but they're a' deid." One Monday morning, during the fishing season, work at the harbour largely came to a standstill while first little groups, then larger ones, discussed Leyton's sermon of the previous day which had been on the subject of conversion. About noon a deputation of three fishermen in their blue jerseys called at the Manse and asked to see the " meenister ". " We didna a'togither like your views on convairsion yesterday," was the burden of their remarks. Our 1 o'clock dinner was very late that Monday, but Leyton ate it with the zest of argument still upon him.

The town might be remote and isolated but it had a fine culture of its own and included a remarkable number of distinguished men among its inhabitants. There was, for example, Mr. W. L. Taylor, the local bookseller and newsagent and one of the deacons of the Congregational Church, who had a unique collection of Scottish Psalters. He would travel anywhere in the British Isles, from Sotheby's to a remote Scottish castle, to acquire a rare Psalter. It was an experience not to be missed to be admitted to his inner sanctum, see the gleam in his eye as he unlocked the glass doors of his book cases, and the reverent caress with which he handled his precious volumes. His collection was bequeathed to the British Museum. His heart was always in that little room, but his daily work, with the help of a young assistant, was selling newspapers and books in his shop, always dressed in a long black frock coat. He was fond of telling how, one day, a breathless small boy rushed in with a penny and panted out, " Gie us a *Christian Wor-rld* and ma Mither sez, if ye hinna yin she'll tak the *Police News*."

Another distinguished inhabitant, Dr. J. F. Tocher, was the owner and dispenser of the local chemist's shop, later to become D.Sc. LL.D., who, beginning with Aberdeenshire, finally carried out an ethnographical survey of the whole of Scotland. Yet another was Lord Catto, who became Chairman of the Bank of England. Peterhead had a good local Choral Society and Literary Society and its townspeople were politically alert, well-informed, and intelligent, and divided between the two main parties.

Leyton, who believed in the principles of Liberalism through all his politically conscious life, was never a mere party man. At a public meeting in 1909 he exasperated many Liberals who were present by strongly criticizing Sir Edward Grey's foreign policy which was the traditional one of Balance of Power in the interests of peace and security. He prophesied that sooner or later it would lead to a European war; that the balance only tempted each side to strive to upset it by becoming the stronger and that not along that path lay peace.

While Leyton was fully occupied in his new sphere I was having a year of leisured activity at home, acquiring a trousseau and household effects, being guided into domestic arts by various friends, playing a little very bad golf, going to a season of Thomas Beecham operas and being the only daughter at home while my sister was working in a Liverpool studio. My brothers came and went, but, except for the youngest, all were now launched on professional careers. Apart from being a regular " twicer " on Sundays the only Church activity I can recall during that year was playing the hymns for Aunt Louie's Women's Bible Class. Looking back it seems a carefree interlude in another world than this, with little responsibility except a leisurely " getting ready to be married ".

One of the interests of the year was hearing Professor George Adam Smith giving four lectures on Jeremiah in Manchester Cathedral and meeting him personally when he and his wife stayed with my people. Canon Hicks, afterwards Bishop of Lincoln, and my father were largely instrumental in arranging for these lectures to be given; in Free Church circles they were looked upon as a landmark, for it was then unprecedented for a non-Anglican to be admitted to a Cathedral pulpit. I remember all the behind-the-scenes discussions as to whether the Professor might be allowed to recite a collect as well as give a lecture, and, if so, where he might be allowed to stand or to kneel. The lectures drew great crowds and were much appreciated. No man was better fitted to cross the barbican with distinction and with dignity than Professor George Adam Smith.

In March 1907, in the early hours of a Sunday morning, my father died of angina; it was my first intimate experience of death. He had worked and preached up to his very last week on earth and as he was a true Father-in-God to his congregation they shared our sense of bereavement. On the morning he died, my mother summed up their marriage in one sentence : " This is the end of thirty-five years of bliss."

Under these circumstances we had a quiet wedding late in August, away from Manchester, where it would have been difficult to keep it so. We were married by my brother Willie in the tiny chapel on the village green at Goathland, Yorkshire, where there was only just room for the near relations and the few friends who were our guests. The chapel was decorated with heather and bracken and no professional hands touched the arrangements. It seemed to fit us better than a more formal ceremony would have done. The wedding breakfast was in the farm house where my family was staying.

We, somewhat improvidently, went to Norway for our honeymoon on the strength of a £50 cheque which an uncle of Leyton's gave us as a wedding present. No one could describe it as the perfect honeymoon. It was late in the season and the rain poured down day after day, but, much more damping than that, the bridegroom developed a heavy cold and a bad sore throat and lost his voice. This was not a passing incident and must be dealt with at some length. Soon after leaving College he had taken part in a friend's ordination while suffering from a severe cold which had almost deprived him of a voice. Whether or not this was the cause, it marked the beginning of throat trouble which was a thorn in the flesh during all his ministerial career. He consulted specialists in many cities and had various courses in voice production. Hardly a year passed without some fresh surgical or medical treatment, including one period of complete silence lasting several months. There was undoubtedly a physical disability which nothing could cure, but it gathered to itself nervous and psychological accompaniments. He dreaded not being able to fulfil public engagements, or not being able to see them through to a finish, and, especially, he feared and disliked speaking engagements away from home. The jarring refrain of " voice trouble " was a constantly recurring one all through his public career, until, when he had finally retired, sore throats

Photo : Edwin Shivas

LEYTON RICHARDS IN HIS FIRST PASTORATE,
PETERHEAD, 1906

[*facing page 36*

mattered no longer. And so, even on our honeymoon, it intruded itself and in the middle of it we left Norway and came back to London for him to take a much advertised course of lessons in voice production, for he was beginning to fear he would be unable to undertake his work after his return. The only complaint I ever heard him utter against Providence was on this subject : " Why has the necessity to preach been laid upon me and such a wretched instrument been given me with which to do it ? " Sometimes when he appeared to be flogging his congregation, one listener at least knew that he was flogging his vocal cords. People who saw his strong, upright frame and were aware of his boundless energy and vigour, hardly realized what a highly-strung man he was, unless they noticed that his slender, well-shaped hands were seldom still, and he was rarely completely relaxed and at rest.

Peterhead gave me a warm welcome but scrutinized me closely to see if I was in any way worthy of their minister. They helped to bring me up in the way I should go, one letting me into the refine-ments of good shortbread, another into properly constituted Scotch broth which should only " smile ", never " laugh " in the pot ; another pointed out that the polish on the outside of the Manse windows was below the recognized standard of our street. They put me to school but they also took me to their kind hearts.

Spring came tardily in that easterly corner of Scotland and soon melted into summer. The tearing gales became breezes, the fierce breakers became smooth, long rollers or even gentle little waves ; the skies lost their banks of dark, swiftly moving clouds and became pale-washed blue, reflected in the sea below. The blue motif was taken up by companies of bluebells (harebells in England) on the tops of the banks by the road sides. At the edges of the golf links were bright patches of bed-straw and ladies' slippers and in the meadows Grass of Parnassus stood up in creamy masses from carpets of golden-red moss.

On an early June morning of such a late spring in 1910 our eldest child was born. Leyton thus announced her coming to a friend : " Miss Margaret Jessica Richards presents her compliments—and howls—to Miss H. Ferguson, and begs to inform her that she and her mother are in flourishing condition."

While she was only a few days old and I was still in bed, a cablegram arrived inviting Leyton to become minister of Collins

Street Independent Church, Melbourne, Australia. For a time all other aspects of the proposal were submerged for me by my conviction that if we went our baby would die of heat in the Red Sea. I have no doubt that, at the moment, subconsciously, I felt I might die there myself—I who always wilt in hot weather. However, with my returning strength, and the reassurances of a children's doctor, I was able to examine the proposition with Leyton dispassionately. When I confided to an old lady that it seemed so far away, she put the matter in proportion by saying, "Far-r frae where?"

Leyton had been four years in Peterhead and the move would not take effect till early in the following year. It seemed the right thing to accept and so, in December 1910, his first pastorate came to an end.

Chapter VII

MELBOURNE

WE SAILED FROM Tilbury in January 1911 by the Orient liner *Orsova* —" we " being Leyton and I, Margaret now in her eighth month, and Lillie Hewart, one who was to become a much valued member of our household for seventeen years, and soon to be known as " Nannie ". She had been a member of my father's Church in Manchester and as my parents, in her eyes, could do no wrong, she was easily persuaded by my mother to go out to Australia with us in a combined capacity of cook and nurse. She was a " good plain cook ", but, more important, she had " a way with children " and her influence on ours was entirely salutary and lasting. She was religious but by no means pious : she had a rich, fruity Lancashire humour, could scent humbug a mile away and wither it with gales of laughter. She had her likes and dislikes and if guests, under the latter category, came to stay her mouth would droop at the corners and her pastry, usually excellent, tended to be a trifle heavy till they had gone. She adopted a body-guard attitude towards us all and would, I am sure, have willingly laid down her life for any of our children. Only the sense of security given by her presence in the background made it possible for me to share as much as I did in the growing responsibilities of Leyton's public work.

We had an altogether enjoyable voyage, going on shore at the usual stopping places and seeing all we could. It was the coolest recorded passage through the Red Sea for many years, so Margaret and I survived it happily.

We sailed into Melbourne in the early hours of a bright and, for Australia, cool February morning and were met by four members of Collins Street Independent Church, including Mr. and Mrs. J. Newman Barker, who, with their two daughters, were to become our near neighbours and our lasting friends. Not a single member of Collins Street Church had seen Leyton when the invitation to become their minister was sent to him, so, prudently, it had been for a year only in the first place ; it was to be reviewed after six months and if not renewed we, with all our goods and chattels, were to be sent home " Carriage Paid ". It was a venture on both sides, for the health and well-being of a Congregational Church— and it must be so of all Churches—depends on a relationship between minister and people of mutual respect and confidence. In Congregationalism both enter into a fellowship of Christian service and witness, by their own choice, seeking divine guidance in the initiation of it and in the maintaining of it, but without submission to any outside authority. It is a method that imposes tests of a high order on both minister and people.

The church was an imposing pile of buildings with a tall campanile and seating capacity for 1,250 people, in the very centre of the city which already had a population of over half a million and which, before the building of Canberra, was the seat of Government of the Commonwealth of Australia. The Federal Parliament, the War Office and other Government Departments were close to the church, and the University not far away. The church premises were well built and extensive, and included the offices of the Congregational Union of Victoria. Each of four denominations had been granted free, large plots of land when the city was originally planned. As the Independent Church had more than enough for its own needs it had built and let a block of offices on its site which brought in a considerable revenue. In contrast, Dr. R. W. Dale of Birmingham, presented with an opportunity for a perpetual endowment of £1,500 when that city was reconstructed, persuaded his fellow trustees at Carrs Lane to forego it except for £480 a year, and transfer the site values to the Scotts Trust, an educational foundation ; it was an act which commended itself to his successor, Leyton Richards, but seldom commends itself to a church treasurer.

Leyton's immediate predecessor at Collins Street was the Rev. Llewelyn Bevan, D.D., who had grown old in the pastorate and had outlived his vigour and his power of holding a large congregation, so that we found an almost empty church when we came. It had in it, however, a sound core of faithful members eager to help in restoring their church to what they believed was its right function, namely to be a preaching and teaching centre, in the midst of a great city to which numbers of men and women could turn for guidance and instruction in the Christian faith. They must have been pleased to see that the church was packed at least for Leyton's Induction, the religious public of Melbourne flocking to see what this new man from England was like and what he had to say. And apart altogether from that occasion we got a characteristically warm-hearted, generous Australian welcome for, to most Australians, England is still "home" though they may never have been there. After a month's residence I remember remarking to Leyton, "Why this is more English than England."

After the first influx of the curious had subsided the hard work of building up a regular congregation began. Leyton's preaching was too solid and closely-knit, and demanded too much of his hearers for him ever to be what is known as a popular preacher, and in fact he never wanted to attract crowds who came and went. He was aware that he had certain gifts which enabled him to speak to large numbers, but he wanted to present them with material which would build up instructed and convinced Christians whose faith would withstand all that could assail it. He had a theory that sermons preached and listened to in the clear light of morning would lay the foundations of a faith which would stand more strain and stress than those which might carry people away in the artificial light and the greater tendency to emotionalism of evening. Not that his preaching ever lacked feeling : it was charged with the passion of deep conviction, but it was conviction arrived at by exhaustive and exhausting thought in his study. And it was conviction, based on reason and reinforced by the emotion of loyalty to truth, which he sought to build up in others. With unremitting faithfulness he carried through his sermon preparation for forty years. He believed that to be worrying about results was none of his business ; faithfulness was within his control, results were not. There is no doubt that he had a deep and lasting influence on a number of thoughtful people, partly because he never feared the findings of science or the most searching Biblical criticism. And why should he? He was convinced that all truth is one, that it comes from God and leads to God and that religion has everything to gain from honest and relentless thought in every realm of knowledge. A stranger coming out of Collins Street Church one Sunday was heard to exclaim : "That's the most honest man who ever stepped into a pulpit."

Such preaching as his, only slowly built up a regular congregation of about five hundred. His influence on these was lasting and, in some cases, transformed an uncertain wavering attitude into firm religious conviction. He never, I suppose, brought about a "sudden conversion" but the fact that he did truly change many people's whole attitude to God and man is established beyond question.

His hearers could not for long imagine that to him Christianity was only a matter of private and personal relationships. He left them in no doubt on that point and soon the city and the Government itself became aware of the presence of a man who believed that "the flaming ethics of Christianity"* applies to public affairs.

With his convictions on the race question, so early inculcated, and later established by reading and by experience, he could not be expected to accept the White Australia policy without examination. He appreciated the manifold difficulties of the problem for a Government charged with the responsibility of preserving the economic and social standards of Australia, which had been so carefully built up. Yet, as he looked at the empty map of the largest island in the world, twice the size of India, with a population then of 4½ million, and looked across at the teeming millions of the Far East, he could not feel that a policy of exclusion was any final solution of a problem which would have to be solved some day or it would submerge the world in the greatest conflict in its history. Race consciousness and pride were growing fast among coloured peoples, at the same time that their death rate was declining and their fecundity increasing. Unless men were wise in time they might as well try to stem Niagara with a dam made of osiers. By no means did he advocate, as an alternative, unrestricted immigration, but with a group of other concerned people he worked out a scheme which might at least have formed a basis for discussion. Short-term policies and expediencies which disregard Christian principles always seemed to him doomed to failure because he regarded those principles as being as much part of the universe as are the laws of chemistry and mathematics. The fact that neither is fully apprehended by man did not seem to him to justify manifest breaches of the principles on the one hand or the "laws" on the other. To disregard them because of a calculation of probable consequences seemed to him to be courting disaster.

An instance of the White Australia policy, as it affected individuals, occurred not long after we got out to Melbourne and it

* Winston Churchill: *The Gathering Storm.*

brought his own views into the limelight. Many years later he wrote an account of the whole incident :

Prior to federation in 1900, a limited number of Chinese were allowed to settle in some of the States, and among such immigrants was a much respected and highly successful merchant in the city of Geelong in the State of Victoria. With the coming of federation, however, coloured immigration was prohibited and this was held to cover the case of children born to non-white parents on Australian soil. Accordingly, when the wife of the Chinese merchant was about to become a mother, an order was made for the repatriation of herself and her husband before the birth occurred. The fact that this would mean the ruin of a business enterprise was not allowed to modify the official decision, and neither was the petition against deportation which was signed by many of the merchant's fellow townsmen. The law must be observed, and preparations were made for the enforcement of the order. I was at that time minister of Collins Street Independent Church in Melbourne and I remember with satisfaction how we organized a meeting of protest against the contemplated act of expulsion. The Anglican Archbishop of Melbourne took the chair, and a resolution was passed and sent to the appropriate Government Department, demanding the immediate cancellation of the order. It is not always that a protest has such an immediate success, but a meeting representative of the city's life and held under the very shadow of the Federal Parliament House could not be ignored. The Press took the matter up in a responsible way, questions followed in the House of Representatives, and before the week was out the offensive and offending order had been rescinded.

Two things are missing from that account of the Poon Gooey Case. One is that, naturally, there is no reference to his own energy in organizing the meeting nor to the forceful eloquence of his own speech. The other is that the harsh treatment of a woman nearing child-birth moved him as well as the ruin of a business.

On the very day on which I began this chapter, April 6th, 1949, a small paragraph appeared in the Press as follows :

A United States negro boxer—Tiger Parkes—was put on board an aircraft here last night for deportation to San Francisco. He had been in prison since March 17th because he refused to obey an order directing him to leave the country where he has lived, in South Australia, with his Australian wife and child, for fifteen years.

The report goes on :

> Last month, Mr. Calwell, Australian Immigration Minister, re-affirmed Australia's policy of excluding non-whites.

On the basis of the draft scheme Leyton worked out, two features at least of this last case would have been absent, for one of its many clauses was to the effect that only *families* and not single men of coloured peoples should be admitted ; a second was that immigrants, for the first generation, should go on the land. I believe that if he were alive to-day he would trace a connection between the rise of Communism in China, in some small part at least, to the White Australia Policy and to incidents such as I have related, for they were widely reported and caused resentment among Eastern peoples. Whatever the sins of the Kremlin, racial discrimination is not one of them. He always believed that only by taking the long and the Christian view could contemporary policies be assessed, and when he used the word "belief" he did literally mean "living by" as he reiterated thousands of times in his preaching.

The White Australia Policy was not the only issue on which Leyton took his stand against the Commonwealth of Australia. A short time before we arrived in Melbourne an amended Defence Bill, based on advice given by Lord Kitchener, had been introduced by the Labour Government then in power and had passed into law. It instituted a deliberately mild form of conscription, designed to be the thin edge of the wedge. Lord Dudley, who was Governor-General at the time, said so, explicitly, when he was back in London :

> He felt sure they would have to increase the length of training . . . but they were right to go slow. It was a bold move to introduce a bill for compulsory training. Compulsion was a thing which many people shied at, but it had been accepted wonderfully well, and it was tactful and politic not to make the term of service too arduous at first, and to let it grow.

The Act provided for ninety hours each year of military training of boys of twelve while still at school ; between fourteen and eighteen they were drafted into the Senior Cadets, with longer hours and days of drill, and from eighteen to twenty-five into the Citizen Forces, where sixteen whole day drills were required each year. Thereafter, they were to be placed in the Reserves till they reached the age of sixty.

It was, indeed, a mild measure, but there were those who not only " shied at " it but were determined to have nothing to do with it at any cost. These included members of the Society of Friends and some others who shared their conviction about war. The slight demands made by the Act, the very few days out of a boy's year required for training justified it to most minds and made them regard any objection to it as irresponsible obstruction and mere scrupulosity. Yet would one offer even half a slice of corned beef to a convinced vegetarian and expect it to be acceptable? Or expect him to take employment in a sausage factory, even if only to scrub the sausage machines?

There were certain provisions in the Act which were specially obnoxious to Quakers and those who shared their convictions about freedom of conscience and war :

> No parent or guardian shall prevent any son or ward who is so serving or liable to serve from rendering the personal service required of him. Penalty one hundred pounds.—Every person, who being a person liable to training . . . fails without lawful excuse to attend a compulsory drill . . . shall be liable to a penalty not exceeding five pounds. . . . In addition, the Court may, if it thinks fit, commit the offender to confinement in the custody of any prescribed authority for such time not exceeding twenty days, as it thinks fit.

The "prescribed authority" for Melbourne defaulters was the Military : the place of detention was the fort at Queenscliff, but when on one occasion two boys escaped, the rest were transferred to an island in Port Philip Bay, whence it was intimated in the public Press, " they would be unlikely to escape as the water was deep and infested with sharks ". Still another clause ran :

> Any member of the Defence Force charged with any offence against this Act may be tried and punished by court-martial or by a civil court.

Those who drew up the Act had foreseen the possibility of con- scientious objection to it and had included certain clauses which they doubtless believed would adequately meet the case. Exemption might be applied for by those " who are forbidden by the doctrines of their religion to bear arms ". . . . " The burden of proving the exemption shall rest on the person claiming the exemption." If the exemption were allowed, then the persons claiming it " shall as far as possible be allotted to non-combatant duties ".

That the defaulters were expected to include mere children on whom would fall the weight of the law was made plain by a clause to the effect that :

> In places where Children's Courts exist, offences against this section committed by cadets under the age of sixteen years shall be prosecuted in such Courts as far as is reasonably practicable.

There were many defaulters, only a few of whom defaulted on grounds of conscience. It was well nigh impossible for any boy outside the Society of Friends, and not always possible within it, to prove to a Court that he was "forbidden by the doctrines of his religion to bear arms". We attended some of the sittings of the Court in which boys appeared. There was present a formidable array of police, representatives of the Military and the Law, and some members of the interested public whose presence, whilst giving support, must have added to the defaulters' embarrassment. The boys themselves presented a picture of mute misery. It was an ordeal indeed to be cross-examined by a magistrate, in public, about religious beliefs, which, if they existed at all, were only in embryo, with parents with consciences listening in the background. There was little sympathy or leniency from the Bench, who showed a tendency to dwell much on " slackers " and " shirkers " and a boy's " debt to the Commonwealth ".

One Quaker family, which had two boys in it, left the country rather than submit. I well remember our seeing them off at the Port of Melbourne and how sad they were to go, as it meant pulling up the roots of a lifetime.

For the most part, the organized religious bodies in Australia seemed unaware of the assault on liberty of conscience involved in the Defence Act, and had accepted it with silent acquiescence. The Society of Friends had made their protest to the Government, but in vain. English Quakers were fully alive to the situation ; J. P. Fletcher and Alfred H. Brown came out from London Yearly Meeting to help.

Leyton's inheritance and training in Nonconformity, in Liberalism, in British tradition and above all in the fundamentals of Christianity, all contributed to his clear conviction on the sovereign rights of conscience, and it followed that the assault on these rights roused him to action. He announced in the Press that on June 16th, 1912, he would preach in Collins Street Independent Church on "Compulsory Military Training and the Duty of the Church. A Plea for Liberty of Conscience." In the crowded church that Sunday were the Minister of Defence and other officials from the War Office. The two texts he chose indicate the kind of sermon it was: "For Zion's sake will I not hold my peace, and for Jerusalem's sake will I not rest," and "Why is my liberty judged by another man's conscience?" What had been described by Professor Raleigh as his "natural oratory" stood him in good stead that evening.

The sermon was afterwards printed and widely circulated. I believe it had no small part in the subsequent passing of resolutions by almost all the religious bodies, asserting their belief in liberty of conscience and their protest against the assault upon it. The Church ought to be outstanding as a "champion of human rights because it stands for the status of man before God."*

Both in this controversy and that on the White Australia Policy, Commonwealth newspapers gave full and fair reports, and especially the *Melbourne Argus* stood magnificently by freedom of the Press, giving much space to these unpopular points of view. A long, spirited, and highly controversial correspondence was printed in the *Argus*, between Leyton and a certain Colonel Crouch, and others.

On the day after the Minister of Defence had listened to this sermon he described it in Parliament as "a seditious utterance", "an indictable offence", but he added that he did not propose to make a martyr of the preacher by prosecuting him. For his own sake I am sure he chose well! In actual fact it was not seditious for it stressed the equal right of conscience of those who believed in conscription and of those who objected on conscientious grounds.

One of the soldiers sent out by the War Office to help to establish compulsory military training was Major Frank Wilson, whose wife happened to be my second cousin. He and others from the British Army were also in Collins Street Church that Sunday night. Some months later I heard their verdict through correspondence from home: "There is only one thing to be said in favour of that man. He is Major Wilson's wife's cousin's husband!" "That man" did

---

* The Bishop of Southwell: *Sunday Times*, March 20th, 1949.

not lose one wink of sleep on account of the turmoil surging round his head. Nor, for that matter, did Major Wilson's wife's cousin.

At about this time an organization called the Australian Freedom League was started with the express object of opposing conscription. Beginning in 1912 with two members in a few years it had 35,000. Compulsory military training did not fit the Australian temperament, quite apart from any conscientious objection to it, and early in 1914 a member of the Federal Parliament stated in the House of Representatives that " the whole system of military drill is fizzling out ". A contributing cause was that education in the Commonwealth was, on the whole, free and liberal in conception and did not match the army method of dealing with adolescents.

One of the provisions of the 1912 Act had been that compulsion was only for purposes of home defence, and this could only be altered by a referendum. When, in October 1916, the Government wished to repeal this limiting clause and submitted the issue to a referendum, even amid the passions of war, the people answered " No." There is no need to remind any one of Australia's contribution to the 1914-18 war in Europe, but the Australians who took part in it came because they chose, not because they must. Later still, in November 1929, the Minister of Defence finally announced that the Cabinet had decided, " for reasons of economy ", to suspend compulsory military training. Some of the nails in its coffin had been hammered in by a handful of Quakers and by Leyton Richards seventeen years earlier.

Those who opposed the Defence Act on conscientious grounds had no less will to defend the highest values of Australian life than those in favour of it. But they saw defence in other terms. They believed, for instance, that a different immigration policy would be more effective than many battalions.

It must not be supposed that all Leyton's time and energy in Melbourne were absorbed in controversy and battles for unpopular causes. There was great exhilaration in the open-air life, tennis all the year round, surf-bathing in warm seas, holidays in the bush, constant sunshine and the friendliness and informality of the people. In the summer of 1913 we had a week's holiday in Tasmania. Part of the British Fleet was in the harbour at Hobart and one afternoon we had tea on board a battle cruiser. There in the officers' mess we heard talk of war with Germany, how it was bound to come and the sooner it came the better. We were hearing the first mutterings of the "gathering storm" of 1914-18; there was no "unpreparedness" in the British Navy, and yet it came.

Soon after this we felt we must decide whether to stay permanently in Australia or to return home. Two considerations chiefly weighed with us. A second daughter, Joyce, had been born to us in 1912 and we had to decide whether we preferred our children to spend their most formative years in an Australian or a British context, both of which have their advantages; the scale dipped on the side of Britain. In the second place we felt that Australia was little touched by some religious and international movements of thought; young and buoyant and adventurous, she lacked the maturity which comes from contact with many nations, though in certain respects she undoubtedly gained by her isolated position. Leyton wanted to be in closer touch, than was possible out there, with Europe and America, with Africans and Indians. At the same time, because Australia soon attaches its immigrants to herself, we felt if we stayed much longer we should find it difficult to leave and should find ourselves out of touch with affairs in England. In August of 1913, therefore, our decision was made and Leyton announced his intention of resigning in the following February, thus giving the Church time to fill his place. How the resignation was received is best told by another pen than mine. The Rev. F. C. Spurr, the well-known English Baptist was for a few years in a church near ours in Collins Street, Melbourne. He wrote an article to the English *Christian World*, from which I quote brief extracts:

Mr. Richards came. He attracted attention immediately. His tall figure, his fresh almost boyish complexion, his captivating stories to the children, his advocacy of all righteous causes, and his virile preaching drew to him some of the best men and women in Melbourne. And now, like a bolt from the blue comes his resignation. . . . And everybody wants to know the reason why. . . . His Church has made a strong attempt to retain him but his decision is final. . . . It will be a heavy loss to a great number of people outside his own communion. . . . For Leyton Richards is a man one cannot help loving. . . . He is a great boy bubbling over with life and fun. That is why he has not a personal enemy in town. . . . Some of Mr. Richards's own people have not been heart and soul with him upon this question (i.e. the Defence Act) but that has nothing whatever to do with his return to England. To a man they are entreating him to remain in Melbourne.

Three small incidents come back to me from the time of our leaving Melbourne. The old Chinese market gardener who called at our house weekly with vegetables and could only speak a few words of English presented us, on parting, with a large table centre of thick beautiful Chinese silk with the words "Good Luck" embroidered in the centre.

Colonel Crouch, with whom Leyton had carried on such prolonged and forthright controversy in the *Melbourne Argus*, was away from Melbourne at the time, but he travelled several hundreds of miles to be present at the farewell meeting in the church.

On the February morning, when our boat sailed at 7 a.m., about two hundred members of the Church were on the quay to see us off. As the boat moved out they sang: "For he's a jolly good fellow." They had been diverted from singing "God be with you till we meet again" at Leyton's request . . . there were so many on that quay whom we should never be likely to meet again on this earth that it would have been a little beyond bearing.

Chapter VIII

SOUTH AFRICA

WE CHOSE TO come home by South Africa so that Leyton could break the journey there for two months. His object was to learn as much as possible in so short a time of African problems and, in particular, of the contribution of the London Missionary Society to their solution. By way of pure holiday and recreation he had planned to see the Victoria Falls in company with two business men friends from England. In the meantime, I was coming straight through to England on the same boat, with the children, though, fortunately, it docked for a few days in Durban and a whole day in Cape Town.

By a fortunate synchronization my brother, W. W. Pearson, whom we had not seen for seven years, was in South Africa when we arrived and was in Durban to meet us. He was there, together with C. F. Andrews, to help Mr. Gandhi in his first trial of the non-violent resistance method of meeting injustice. The Indian population was suffering intolerable legalized indignities at the hands of the Government and had appealed to their Motherland to send help ; freedom of movement within the Union was denied to Indians. Now that India has self-government she is said to be retaliating and it is reported that South African sightseers and tourists are not allowed to visit the Taj Mahal. If it is true, they have no right to complain. My brother had already been in South Africa for several months when we landed and was immersed in the cause of justice for the Indian. The day after we arrived Leyton and I went with him to a meeting of the Indian Women's Passive Resistance Association presided over by an Indian woman : a presentation was made to him in gratitude for his work for their community and all three of us were garlanded. Because of our relationship to him we came in for some reflected glory, and, when the children and I left a few days later, there were great baskets of fruit and flowers in my cabin, sent by the Indian community. As soon as we had sailed, Leyton and Willie went on to Phoenix, an Indian Agricultural Settlement founded by Mr. Gandhi. Leyton kept a diary of the whole of his South African tour and posted it to me in instalments, and extracts from it are the best record I can give.

FEB. 23RD. All non-Europeans in Durban confined on trams to two back seats on top; W.W.P. reported cases of ill-treatment by conductors, e.g. Indian woman with basket of crockery placed basket on rear platform of tram: conductor kicked it off on to the road: consequent breakage and loss.

FEB. 24TH. W.W.P. and I went by train to Phoenix, an Indian industrial and agricultural settlement founded by Mr. M. K. Gandhi. The settlement three miles from the station. . . . Arrived soaked through with rain and perspiration to find the Community at evening worship. Thirty of them, all ages, both sexes. Portions of sacred scriptures were read, and Hindu hymns sung: also " Lead Kindly Light " in English. . . . Evening meal of unleavened bread and strange Indian dishes of meal and fruit: strictly vegetarian. Not palatable to an unaccustomed tongue, but did my best! W.W.P. ate with gusto. . . . In the absence of Mr. M. K. Gandhi, his brother, Mr. C. K. Gandhi, was in charge.

FEB. 26TH. Reached Johannesburg at 6 p.m. Natives, Indians and coloured people not allowed on the pavements, trams, or in the public parks. . . . The natives struck me as defiant compared with those in Durban. They swagger as they walk, and groups of them will stand just off the pavement and jeer at the white passers-by, laughing uproariously at little peculiarities of gait or costume, and sometimes imitating them.

FEB. 27TH. Went to see Mr. ——, Manager and part proprietor of the British S. African —— Company. He has made great sacrifices on behalf of the natives and coloured people, having been pushed out of public life and suffered in his private concerns for his sympathies. . . . He, like practically every friend of the Native I have met, condemns most severely the Boer attitude and thinks Union a bad thing for the Native. Prior to Union the Boer Government was confined to the Boer territories: now the Boer controls the whole country. As one result the Native Congress which used to meet in Johannesburg under Lord Milner . . . is this year forbidden by General Botha under martial law and so is forced to assemble in Kimberley, which is right out of the way, but where martial law is not in operation. . . .

LEYTON AND EDITH RICHARDS WITH MARGARET AND JOYCE,
MELBOURNE, 1912

[facing page 52

In speaking of the native question and trying to draw men on the subject in trains, hotels, etc., I am impressed with the complete absence of thought or policy upon what is undoubtedly *the* problem of South Africa and by the side of which in the long run all questions of Labour and Capital, Boer and British, Asiatic and Imperial, must sink into comparative insignificance. Even statesmen seem to have no other idea but that of white dominance, alike political and economic, and however secured. . . . The very remoteness of the problem in an acute form seems, in the minds of most whites, to absolve them from all responsibility in regard to the Native ; and yet obviously, wisely to determine now the lines that will best conduce to the ultimate welfare of both races, will make all the difference to the weal and woe of S. Africa. Present methods are merely a foolish amalgam of selfishness and drift, and some day there must be a terrible harvest. . . .

MARCH 2ND. Arrived at Kimberley. . . . Attended the Native National Congress. . . . Called on unexpectedly to address the delegates, and reporters were present : two native languages—Bechuana and Zulu—were necessary, and so I was followed sentence by sentence by a couple of interpreters. This does not conduce to flights of oratory but it enables one to weigh one's words before uttering them. . . . A good report next morning in *The Diamond Fields Advertiser*. . . .

The main business before the Congress was the Land Act just passed, and its bearing upon Native life. This has roused a great deal of resentment, as the Natives were not consulted before the Bill was passed and it vitally affects their future. An appeal to Botha as Prime Minister has met with the usual curt " non possumus ", and so the Congress decided to send a deputation to the King, which is the Natives' explicit right under the Union Constitution. Tactically, however, it is likely to be unavailing as the Home Authorities would hardly interfere with a self-governing dominion in respect of an Act duly passed : it would have been better to wait until administrative hardships accumulated under the Act and then appeal to the King as Protector of the Natives. . . . One or two members expressed themselves as doubtful of the success of the deputation . . . the President and officers in particular warning the members not to be disappointed at failure, and indeed to go back to the tribes and prepare them for such an eventuality. This declaration led one member (who spoke English well) to threaten a Native rebellion (with hints as to rifles already prepared) if the King refused to act. " Then we will say to Great Britain, we have done with

Great Britain: we will say to the Union of South Africa, we have no further need of you: you have betrayed us: the King has failed us: we will gather our chiefs and raise our own flag, and live as we have a right to live who were here before the white man came." Wild talk, fiercely applauded, though disowned by the leaders; but it is a symptom: the policy of suppression and exploitation of the natives in the interests of the white man is having its inevitable reaction in the creation of violent unrest and seditious talk. . . .

The debating power of the Native is a very marked faculty: due to the absence of literature, memoriter work has been highly developed, and this enables them without note or reminder to reply at length to previous speakers. An excellent instance of this was Mr. Dube's [President of Native Congress, educated in America] reply to Mr. Dower, the Permanent Secretary for Native Affairs under the Union Government . . . sent by General Botha to represent the Government at the Congress. . . . Mr. Dower devoted the main part of his address to the delegates to a defence of the Land Act. . . . When he sat down after forty-five minutes, Dube immediately rose, and point by point, without a note, followed him through his speech and, as far as I could judge, left him without a leg to stand on. It was certainly one of the ablest debating speeches I ever listened to (spoken in English for Dower's benefit): entirely extempore, eloquent, reasoned, and with a wealth of facts marshalled with telling precision. . . .

MARCH 3RD. Left Kimberley. . . . Arrived Tiger Kloof (an institution founded and maintained by the London Missionary Society), was guest of Organe. Called on Mr. Willoughby, the Principal. The Institution is a most impressive sight as one approaches by rail . . . neat, orderly, well-built, fenced and laid out . . . everything has been done on the spot, from the quarrying of the stone to the weathercock on the tower, as part of the industrial training which the students receive. . . . It is a practical recognition of the fact that the modern missionary problem is on one side a vast social problem : how to fit the Native to take his place adequately and without disaster to himself in the new social environment created by the introduction and spread of a European civilization. To that problem Tiger Kloof is the answer—or the beginning of an answer. The Native can never be more than an economic tool exploited by the more civilized race, unless he, too, is taught to use his innate capacities and control them, as they develop, by the highest Christian impulses. . . . There has been real statesmanship in the creation of the Institution, and to talk with Mr. Willoughby is to discover the Statesman.

54

MARCH 9TH-13TH. At Victoria Falls. The barman came on to the veranda of the Hotel one evening, rubbing his hands, and with voluble curses declared that he was quite sore with thrashing some niggers. I found later in Bulawayo that the flogging of " Boys " is now prohibited in Rhodesia, since two died from flogging a couple of years ago ; but it still goes on, and the Native is too ignorant to obtain legal redress. . . . The average colonial type met on trains and in hotels does not impress one as of the kind to solve the Native problem, but rather to aggravate it. Talk to him, and he will tell you that " Niggers " are just children and must be treated as such . . . true enough to fact if only the whites would act, truly, *in loco parentis*. Children call for education and patient training, for discipline in the true sense, and the crack of the whip in the hands of a bully is no instrument for that. . . .

MARCH 15TH. On my journey . . . the train stopped for twenty minutes : I walked back to the car for Natives which is always an interesting sight as local Natives seem to spring out of the veldt at every stopping place and hold confab with the travellers. . . . One of the men (in the Native car) was a Wesleyan teacher and preacher . . . who knew [two L.M.S. missionaries I had met]. The man had his wife with him and a baby just under two, which was puling and restless : we had then come six hours in the boiling heat and the child had not slept, for the conductor refused to let the man have any water to soak the mealie bread which was the baby's food. So I took the man's billy and filled it with water at the dining saloon filter and told the conductor what I had done : he merely laughed and said that niggers were quite used to going without water. At the next stop I went back again to see how they were getting on. It was dark, being about 9 p.m. and yet the Natives' car was without light. I asked the conductor if that was the usual case, and he said the dynamo under the car was out of order : so there was an end of it. Five minutes later some baggage had to be stowed in the car and immediately the light was switched on !

The diary goes on to tell of his visits to Tiger Kloof and his meeting with Chief Khama before whom he preached one Sunday as he sat on a carved stool in the open air in front of a congregation of 2,000. At the end of the service the great Chief presented the preacher with the stool on which he had been sitting and the horse's tail mounted in a carved handle with which he had kept off the flies : they are still treasured possessions. He had many visits to missionaries, attended sittings of Parliament in session in Cape Town and finally left for home on April 4th.

His diary is thirty-five years old, and may be regarded as out of date, but its interest lies in the fact that to-day " the air is thick with chickens coming home to roost ".*

He brought home with him a copy of the inscriptions on two South African monuments. The first, to the twenty-six thousand Boer women and children who died in British concentration camps during the Boer War, 1899-1902 : " As your tribute to the dead, bury unforgiveness and bitterness at the foot of this monument for ever. Forgive, for you can afford it, the rich who were greedy of more riches, the Statesmen who could not guide affairs, the bad generalship that warred on weaklings and babes—forgive."

The other, a monument unveiled in 1912 to commemorate three people who lie buried there, a Boer President, Steyn ; a Boer General, de Wet ; an English woman, Emily Hobhouse, who, in the words of General Smuts at her funeral, by reason of her efforts to relieve the distress and suffering of the prisoners, " became the great symbol of reconciliation between peoples who should never have been enemies ".

---

* Said by a Chinese to the Assembly of the League of Nations, when the war clouds were gathering over East and West, referring specially to its passivity with regard to the Manchurian invasion.

Chapter IX

BOWDON, CHESHIRE, 1914-1916

WITHIN A MONTH of his return to England in April 1914, Leyton was invited to address the Yearly Meeting of the Society of Friends in London, that they might hear his account of the opposition to the Australian Defence Act. The Free Church Council of Great Britain also invited him to preach at their Annual Meetings and his sermon, which was a call to the Church to stand for peace and freedom of conscience, was received with approbation and even with enthusiasm. He had never held an English pastorate and was not well known through work in England, but reports of his witness for freedom of conscience in Australia had travelled home before him and had been approved in his own denomination and in the Free Churches generally. In the spring of 1914 the atmosphere of the home Churches was strongly pacific though not pacifist.

Among engagements during June he preached one Sunday at Bowdon Downs Congregational Church, eight miles out of Manchester on the Cheshire side. Its best-known minister had been Dr. Alexander Mackennal, the impress of whose teaching and personality was still on the Church. Its pastorate was vacant at this time and Leyton was invited to fill it and to begin his ministry on the first Sunday in September. They knew of and approved the stand he had taken in Melbourne. Between the acceptance of the invitation and his induction war was declared. During the last days of July and the first of August Leyton hurled himself with all his strength against the decision to go to war and at the very moment when Asquith was speaking in the House of Commons, he was addressing a crowded peace meeting in the Milton Hall, Manchester. Friends of ours, at that time on a motor tour through Europe, were racing across Germany, in order not to be trapped there for the duration of the war. They told us how in towns through which they passed there were large demonstrations of people demanding peace—the counterpart of many such in England.

Before we got to Bowdon most of the young men in the Church had already joined up ; other members of the congregation were almost all gradually absorbed into war work of various kinds : Mr. Faulkner Armitage, Mayor during the war years of the Court Leet of Altrincham and Bowdon, and his wife, were prominent in all work calculated to keep up the morale of the troops and the civil population. Sir Arthur Haworth, an ex-junior Lord of the Treasury, Chairman of Governors of the Manchester Grammar School and Major in the Volunteer Cheshire Regiment, threw himself whole-heartedly into the organization of Home Defence. Many of the women of the Church gave their time to a most efficient voluntary War Supply Depot for making everything needed for the wounded : as the war progressed it worked both day and night shifts. After a time two large houses in Bowdon were lent by their owners as hospitals and other Church members became nurses, orderlies and domestic workers in them. Others were caring for sick horses in Blue Cross work. The speed, efficiency and reliability of all this work was most impressive : with quiet determination and con-trolled emotion, which was neither visible nor vocal, even when their men began to be reported killed or missing, each carried through his or her appointed task. Had we felt able to throw ourselves wholeheartedly into the war effort beside them we should have enjoyed a rich comradeship.

The Australian Defence Act had forced Leyton to think out his position with regard to Christianity and war. He was convinced that, however noble the motives of war might be, its methods were contrary to the life and teaching of Jesus Christ and that it was the duty of the Church to stand true to their professed faith in Him as the Way, the Truth and the Life, and that to do otherwise was to becloud and indeed to jeopardize her witness to Christianity in the world from which she would soon become indistinguishable. He had no use for appeasement but held that the Christian way of meeting evil was to stand firmly by righteousness and at the same time to oppose evil by good. He trusted that thus dealing with an enemy might dissolve his enmity and turn evil to good, but he knew it might not be so ; yet he believed that it was still the course which a man or a nation professing to be Christian ought to take. He recognized that such a course might lead to temporal disaster as it had led Christ Himself to the Cross, but that Christianity would only triumph in the end if men were true to it, whatever the consequences : that the only way of defending Christianity was to be Christian, and, however splendid the motives, he could not believe that to bayonet, to bomb, to blast and to blockade, innocent and guilty alike, came within the sanctions of Christianity.

As far as Leyton knew in the early months of the war, apart from members of the Society of Friends, he held these views in almost complete isolation. In December 1914 he received an invitation from Henry T. Hodgkin, Quaker, doctor and missionary, to attend a conference in Cambridge on the subject of Christianity and War. He went a depressed and lonely man and came back a few days later transfigured, for he had found 130 people who thought as he did and they had together brought into being the Fellowship of Reconciliation on a Christian pacifist basis. Later the F.O.R. gathered to itself many adherents, in many countries east and west, north and south, and it has had much influence. A branch of it came into being soon afterwards in Bowdon itself where it still functions.

So long as he remained in the ministry and occupied a pulpit each Sunday, Leyton conceived it as his first duty to preach Christianity as he understood it : he believed that the Church was guilty of a denial of her faith by supporting the war, its members having failed to distinguish between ends and means. It had never been a temptation to him to please or flatter a congregation : he enjoyed his own powers of advocacy too much and in any case he was a born fighter. But now, for the first time, he found it difficult to obey the injunction to a prophet : Be not afraid of their faces. For the faces upon which he looked down from his pulpit each Sunday were those of men and women burdened with anxiety, and giving their all to a cause which they believed wholly righteous—a war " to uphold the sanctity of treaties ", " to make the world safe for democracy ", and, above all, " a war to end war ". There was indeed a small group of staunch pacifists but most members of the Church were completely absorbed in the war, and so, in a different way, was their minister. He engaged in much controversy on the war issue during this time in the *Manchester Guardian* and the *Christian World*. Once he made the mistake of using the name of the Church as his address but some members, through one of the deacons, pointed out what a mistake it had been and it was never

repeated.   Week by week the congregation was called upon to listen
to sermons and Bible passages in which a pacifist interpretation of
Christianity was often explicit but always implicit.   He had no wish
to be entrenched in a pulpit where he could not be answered and he
announced week-night conferences where members, perforce silent
on Sundays, could put the other point of view, but I doubt if any
minds were changed thereby or any positions much modified.
Sometimes Leyton deliberately tried to give the subject a Sunday
rest.   I remember one week in particular when he told me on
Monday morning he felt the congregation had just about reached
the limit of endurance and that he intended to preach the following
Sunday on a subject remote from the controversial issue and had
chosen the Parable of the Ten Virgins.   On Thursday a worried
face appeared at the dining room door with, " Could you possibly
come and listen to something in the study? "   " Something " was
a half-made sermon : I listened and there was the perennial issue of
war and peace sticking right up in the very centre of the bridal
procession of virgins.   How he found it there I can no longer
remember but at the time it seemed that it certainly *was* there and
could not be banished into silence without dishonour.   So there was
no rest for the congregation after all.   Another Sunday when the
British blockade of Germany had become one of Britain's most
effective weapons, he read the 12th chapter of Romans.   He read
well and people always listened closely to the lessons.   His voice
went on pleadingly : " Recompense to no man evil for evil.   Provide
things honest in the sight of all men.   If it be possible, as much as
lieth in you, live peaceably with all men.   Dearly beloved, avenge
not yourselves, but rather give place unto wrath, for it is written
Vengeance is mine : I will repay, saith the Lord.   Therefore if
thine enemy hunger " . . . then came a pause and swift anger
suddenly shook him, and he ended—" *starve 'em out !* "

" Woe is unto me if I preach not the Gospel " was the inner
compulsion driving him on and the more he became aware of the
growing opposition in the Church the more strained and harsh he
became.   " Why must he strafe us so? " murmured one member as
she left the church after a service.   An old friend of mine, spending a
week-end with us, said after a Sunday morning : " He's dead right,
but if I had a son in the trenches I should want to kill him."

Many members of the congregation must have been tried and

exasperated beyond measure : some left, though a few, because of his attitude, came : but the strain and conflict for him also were immeasurable. Once a mother came on a Saturday morning to say that her son was home from France on leave : could Leyton refrain from references to the war next day as her boy needed strength and comfort not the planting in his mind of doubts and uncertainties? Or Lord Kitchener's death by drowning was the outstanding war news one Saturday : "They will expect me to preach about him to-morrow," said Leyton, "and I am not going to. How much does his death hinder the coming of the Kingdom of God?" Or a letter came from an old friend in London whose only son had been killed at the front. "I cannot admit into my mind one thought which would belittle his sacrifice." Truly there are vested interests in war whose value is unpriced.

It was not, however, all opposition that he met. Reference has already been made to the group which emerged inside the Church and formed themselves into a branch of the Fellowship of Reconciliation. Support came in other strange and unexpected ways. A small boy, taunted by another at having " a — pacifist " as his minister, took off his coat and engaged in a hand-to-hand fight, in the school playground, in which blood flowed. In 1916 Nannie, more than ever regarding herself as a bodyguard, out for a walk with the children, confronted a lady who was prominent in the Church with : "Why can't you all leave Mr. Richards alone? He's the best man I know." Within the home her admiration was less pronounced : after a long grim silence, she attacked him one day with some violence : "Can't you put your conscience to sleep till Mrs. Richards has had her baby?" As it would have meant putting the conscience into cold storage for several months and consciences so treated are apt to remain permanently frost-bitten, there could be only one answer. Soldiers were more inclined to agree with him than civilians. One, quite outside Church circles, said : "You don't mean to say that the people in your Church think war is Christian? They'd get no one in the army to agree with them. Of course it isn't. Christianity is a beautiful ideal but quite impracticable." And another : "I know now that you are right. I was all confused when I joined up and I went to my minister for advice : he talked with me and prayed with me, so I'm in khaki, but after what I've seen I would be a C.O. if I had the guts."

We found great comfort at this time in reading the life of William Lloyd Garrison and being reminded that " the world of politics is always twenty years behind the world of thought . . . and lives and works in ideals which are twenty years old ".   And that the anti-slavery movement in America had also rent the Churches and found them almost entirely pro-slavery, and that " all association " —ecclesiastical as well as political—" is opposed to any disrupting idea ".   And, most cheering of all, " An evil reaches its climax at the very moment that the corrective reform is making a hidden march upon it from an unexpected quarter."

We were often urged to take our share in war-work of a humanitarian kind : but we felt there was other work which needed to be done with less people willing to do it.   Germans were being turned adrift and homeless till they could arrange to get back to Germany. One of these, a girl, stayed with us for several months.   An elderly German lady who had lived and taught in Bowdon for thirty years began to attend the Church, but one day she called on us to say goodbye.   She said : " I do harm to you by coming to your church : you are being called pro-Germans : I do harm to all my friends by knowing them : so I am going back to Germany where I shall be home-sick and lonely all the time.   I no longer belong anywhere."

The Society of Friends and the Fellowship of Reconciliation in Manchester, in 1915, collected money to buy every child of an interned German in the district a shilling Christmas present.   It fell to my lot to deliver two of these at a house in Bowdon.   The Austrian father of the family, an able scientist, was working while in internment for the British Government.   I was received by his wife, a well-dressed woman, in a well-furnished drawing-room.   When I had explained why I had come and handed her the two cheap gimcrack toys, she began to cry.   Then, quickly pulling herself together, she said : " Please excuse me but the children and I are so lonely."

We had much contact with conscientious objectors at this time. There was a small group of them who met in Bowdon, but many more in Manchester where periodic meetings of the No-Conscription Fellowship, with some outstanding speaker from London, were inspiring occasions when we felt we really were pioneers in a coming world movement to abolish war.   I remember especially a meeting where the Chairman, Clifford Allen, later Lord Allen of Hurtwood, warned men not to join the movement unless they were prepared for imprisonment, ostracism, sacrifice of all worldly prospects, and death itself. This was no idle warning for all these might lie ahead of conscientious objectors in the 1914-18 war. Thirty-four, drafted out to France in the army, having failed to convince their tribunals of the sincerity of their conscientious objection, were sentenced by Court Martial to be shot, though, owing to eternal vigilance, a question was asked in Parliament just in time to save them, and their sentences were commuted to ten years' penal servitude.

As we left the brightly lighted hall with the unaccustomed comradeship, and went out into the dark and murky Manchester streets, it was in an exalted mood that we said good-night to each other. But next day, for most pacifists, instead of the challenge of " blood, toil, tears and sweat " there were only pin-pricks—A psychologist gave it as his considered opinion that physical fear was the sub-conscious motive behind pacifism (he did not generalize as to the sub-conscious motives behind soldiering) ; or one would be cut by an acquaintance in the street. But many faced worse than pin-pricks, e.g. one boy had to leave home because his parents were so ashamed of him. One C.O. was forsaken by his young wife who could stand him no longer and left him, with a white feather for remembrance.

Many conscientious objectors came to see Leyton. They were of all kinds, some were large-minded idealists ; some, tiresome individualists ; some were intellectually able, strong, clear, and confident as to their duty ; others were weak, muddle-headed, and incapable of standing up to argument, yet groping their way to a position they *felt* to be right. The less certain ones were apt to present to the world a jaunty air which soon dropped away when they were among friends : they were usually those who had suffered most from relations and companions : they walked through the world unsustained by understanding, unsupported by approbation. When such as these came to see Leyton, after a time, sounds of cheerful laughter would come from the study and it seemed to me that they walked down our garden path with firmer step and shoulders squared.

Leyton had been a member of the No-Conscription Fellowship and its Committee since its inauguration, though he resigned in the spring of 1916 as he did not entirely agree with some points in its general policy. Before his resignation he had signed a leaflet called " Repeal the Act ", protesting against the Conscription Act passed early in 1916 : it was signed by the eight members of the Committee, including three Quakers. On May 10th, 1916, each of the eight was summoned to appear before the Court of Summary Jurisdiction at the Mansion House on a charge of prejudicing recruiting and military discipline. The two policemen responsible for Leyton's appearance in court, saw him to London Road Station, Manchester, and then said rather bashfully : " We think, Sir, it would be best if we travelled up by the other line and we will meet you at Euston." So a good journey was had by all.

There was not much room for the public in the small court where the trial was heard.* Bertrand Russell and Mrs. Despard had managed to get in, and there were press men everywhere in any space they could find. Mr. Clifford Allen, Chairman of the Fellowship, and Lord Derby, Director-General of Recruiting, shared a bench. The words *Deus dirige nos* were carved on the back of the dark oak chair occupied by Sir Alfred Newton, the magistrate hearing the case. Mr. Bodkin appeared for the prosecution and in opening his case quoted a sentence from the leaflet : " Conscription involves the sub-ordination of civil liberties to military dictation "— he went on : " That is not only false it is mischievous. . . . The Tribunals are democratic and popular. . . . It is the highest form of freedom to allow a man to fight for his country in a war which if waged unsuccessfully may be disastrous to his country." "War which is wrong . . ." he read from the leaflet ; then, pausing and fixing his eye on the magistrate, he reached his most compelling argument. " Suppose this view were held generally, there would be no men to carry on war either offensive or defensive. War would become impossible if all men held the view that war is wrong." The accused men smiled. Lord Derby gave evidence, and asked by the magistrate, though Defending Counsel protested, whether in his *opinion* the leaflet would be likely to prejudice recruiting, he expressed his opinion that it would. General Childs came next : he was in charge of the disciplinary work of the army and dealt with reports of all Courts Martial dealing with C.O.s. He considered that the influence

* I owe many of the details of the trial to a contemporary account of it by Mr. Fenner Brockway.

of the leaflet would be entirely subversive. Asked if he knew any Quakers, he replied, "I am glad to say I don't."

The Defence was largely based on an assurance given by Mr. Herbert Samuel in the House of Commons in January that year, as follows :

> Meetings which are limited to opposition to the passing of the Military Service Bill or to advocating its repeal if passed into an Act, or to any opposition to any extension of Compulsory Service, and writings of the same character would not be liable to suppression.

The Quaker, Edward Grubb, was the first defendant to give evidence. He gave his answers in the witness box, quietly, true to Quaker tradition, and some present felt they were indeed back in the days of religious persecution if such as he were regarded by the State as a criminal. Cross-examined by Mr. Bodkin, he was asked if he knew that branches of the No-Conscription Fellowship were coming into being in guard-rooms : "No, but I approve of it," he said unwaveringly, "and it is exactly what my Quaker ancestors did in the seventeenth century."

Leyton was the last witness ; after stating his experiences in Australia as his reason for signing the leaflet, he went on, according to a Press report of that time :

> "I signed the leaflet as a Christian man. Jesus Christ was the Prince of Peace." "Others speak of the God of Battles," commented Mr. Bodkin. "Not in the New Testament," replied Mr. Richards. "The Bible says 'An eye for an eye and a tooth for a tooth.'" "Kindly finish the quotation," said Mr. Richards. "Do you remember that Jesus Christ said 'Render unto Caesar the things that are Caesar's'?" asked the presiding magistrate. "Yes, 'and *unto God* the things that are God's'," Mr. Richards responded with a swiftness which took the magistrate's breath away. "I do not think we had better discuss theology further," he remarked.

Sentence was passed, the maximum penalty being imposed of £100 on each of the eight defendants, with £10 costs or sixty-one days' imprisonment in default of distress. The defendants enjoyed the description of themselves in the *Daily Express* next day in the headline, "'Pasty Faces' convicted." They appealed to Quarter Sessions and were heard at the Guildhall on June 28th. General Childs was again a witness for the prosecution and said it would be a good thing for the discipline of the army if the conscientious objectors were eliminated from it, but his way of eliminating them was to shoot them. When pressed on this point he said this was his *theoretical* view. The defendants' case was strengthened by the fact that one of their number, Councillor Morgan Jones, had to be brought out of Cardiff gaol to attend. He was there undergoing a sentence of four months' imprisonment for refusing to obey military orders. He was attended by two policemen and looked worn and ill, but he gave his answers with great spirit. He had been in solitary confinement for three weeks. The Mansion House decision was upheld.

On the same day, also at the Guildhall, Bertrand Russell's appeal was being heard against an identical sentence for a leaflet he had published defending a C.O. called Everett for refusing to obey military orders. On the wall facing the magistrate in this court were the words *Audi Alteram Partem.*

At the very moment when these cases were being heard in London, the anti-Militarist, Dr. Karl Liebknecht, was being tried in Germany. June 28th, 1916, is a date to be remembered in the annals of anti-militarism.

Both the Mansion House and Guildhall trials were held in full publicity, and all involved in them were prominent men well able to defend themselves. And yet, reading the press reports after more than thirty years, I think no one could regard them as free from prejudice and war-mindedness on the part of the prosecutors. Even less unprejudiced were many of the happenings at the Tribunals, where obscure, often almost speechless, conscientious objectors had to convince unsympathetic men of their sincerity.

The day after Leyton got home from the Appeal, three deacons from Bowdon Downs Church called : he thought at once that a last straw had broken the camel's back, and now the resignation which he had offered several times during the past twenty-two months was going to be accepted. What then was his surprise when they handed him an envelope which contained a cheque for £100 to meet his fine! Strain in the Church had been great but it had never become friction : profound difference had never become intolerance : there had been imperfect appreciation of the views held by each side in the controversy but mutual respect had survived. At the same time, Leyton felt that the breaking point would soon come and he wrote a letter to the Church members resigning :

As I look round from the pulpit, I am not blind to the condition of the Church, nor are my ears deaf to the criticism that reaches me through various channels. I receive letters of remonstrance and appeal, and I cannot but be aware of the disintegrating effect of my preaching on the congregation generally. Reluctantly, but decidedly, I am driven to the conclusion that, with individual exceptions, the Church of Jesus Christ to-day receives the message of " Peace and Goodwill " with pain, and unless the preacher will qualify the message in favour of the present war, his ministrations are a constant irritant and an unwelcome infliction.

I do not complain of the attitude adopted by those to whom I refer. On the contrary, I bear witness to their consistent courtesy to me personally, and to the truly Christian forbearance which they have exhibited in their attitude to " liberty of prophesying ". I am conscious of no attempt forcibly to abridge this liberty ; but I know that so long as I exercise it in fidelity to Christian Truth, as I conceive it, worship is impossible to many of my hearers, and the Sunday services embitter rather than bless.

I am often asked why I cannot let disputed questions alone. I wish I could. But so long as I am set to preach the Gospel of the Prince of Peace, I cannot. To me war and the situations incidental to it, are such a flagrant challenge to my whole conception of Christianity that silence on my part in regard to these things would be infidelity to One whom I call Lord and Master. . . .

I need not elaborate the case. You will see that I am " in a strait betwixt two ". . . . I see but one exit. I must seek outside the ministry of this Church that opportunity which I cannot honourably find within it, of bearing witness to the faith I hold.

They, too, agreed that the time had come for him to go but they proposed that he should still remain their minister and be given leave of absence for the duration of the war and serve in the Friends' Ambulance Unit, while they continued to support his family. He had, at the outbreak of war, considered offering himself to the F.A.U., but had decided then, and was still of the same mind, that he was called upon to make a more outspoken protest against war than was explicit, though it was implied, in such service.

His resignation therefore stood.

As I return in thought to those years 1914-16 in Bowdon, I seem to hear voices battering all the time, a confusion of voices, always voices, voices, voices.

Chapter X

HITHER AND THITHER,
AND BOWDON AGAIN

IT WAS WITH a sense of relief and having laid down a burden that we sat down to supper after Leyton's last Sunday service in Bowdon on July 30th, 1916. We were not, however, to be left for long in a state of quiescence. Early next morning his call-up papers for the army were delivered at the house. Then someone else went on the war-path on behalf of this arch-pacifist. Sir Arthur Howarth had been one of those who found attendance at Bowdon Downs under Leyton's pacifism insupportable. He had been a loyal member and Church officer there for many years, but he was now to be seen on Sundays at the neighbouring Anglican Church, St. Margaret's. Whether he found much satisfaction in the change I do not know, for the incumbent was Canon Hewlett Johnson, now "the Red Dean", who was also a pacifist but of a milder and more benign variety than Leyton. Sir Arthur himself was, in any case, no militarist and became, in later years, a pillar of the League of Nations Union. At this time his only son was in the fighting forces and he and his family were prominent in the war effort. He was a Liberal and Nonconformist to the marrow and, above all, a staunch Congregationalist. He was, therefore, greatly incensed when news of Leyton's having been called up reached his ears. It implied that Free Church ordination and ministry were less valid than Anglican, where no clergyman, whether in a charge or not, was liable for military service. "Once a clergyman or minister always a clergyman or minister" should, he believed, apply all round or not at all. He, therefore, took up the cudgels with the local Recruiting Officer and afterwards got a question asked in Parliament, and answered to his satisfaction. Thereafter no Free Church minister temporarily out of a charge could be called up. It was a strange involuntary gift to come through a pacifist to his brother ministers, especially as he used to say that if he believed in the cause and the urgency of fighting for it as wholeheartedly as most of them did, he would have been at the front and not in a pulpit. He never could see any higher obligation than was laid on a man by calling himself a Christian whatever his place in life. If it was unfitting for a parson to fight because of his *profession*, it seemed just as unfitting for a Christian to fight because of his *professions*.

Leyton's resignation was announced in the Press and among many other letters brought two which touched us much. Dr. Rendel Harris, at that time Curator of MSS. at the Rylands Library, Manchester, wrote offering the hospitality of his home to Leyton and his family as long as it should be needed. The other came from a Quaker business man in Manchester saying that he would make a place for a clerk in his office if Leyton had nothing better in view. Though we did not need to accept either of these offers we greatly appreciated their kindness. Our relations and various friends, whether they agreed with us or not—and some did, some didn't—would never have seen us homeless. Our immediate plan was for the two children, Nannie and me, to go to my mother's house the other side of Manchester and to stay there till after our third child was born. In the meantime Leyton was to go to the Pilgrim Church, Brooklyn, New York, and fill the pulpit there for five months till their prospective minister, Dr. Richard Roberts, Secretary of the British Fellowship of Reconciliation, could take up his appointment with them. America was not yet in the war and Leyton still believed that she could render better service and shorten the war as a great neutral and possible negotiator than as a partici-pant. He spoke at meetings in many places and realized after a time that a detective from the British Government was always present. As he had nothing to hide he was glad to see him there : the man always left as soon as Leyton had spoken. At one point the British Ambassador, Sir Cecil Spring-Rice, through an official representative in Philadelphia, expostulated with him for spreading false information about his own country. Leyton had been warning audiences of the kind of thing liable to happen under Conscription, and had cited the death sentence passed by a Court Martial in France on thirty-four conscientious objectors. He was able to supply the Ambassador with exact information including the names of the thirty-four men and the dates in *Hansard* when the matter was brought before the House and the death sentence commuted to ten years' penal servitude. With the Ambassador's permission, the letter containing these facts was communicated to the Press, which had given publicity of a rather sensational order to the original statement: it was written in conjunction with the well-known Quaker, Prof. Rufus Jones of Haverford. Sir Cecil Spring-Rice wrote a personal letter to Leyton withdrawing his accusations of bad faith.

In a dense fog on a Sunday night in January 1917, Leyton got back to Liverpool and, always quick in his movements, and well used to landing from America, was among the first to leave the boat. He came on to Manchester to my mother's house and was there introduced to his two months old youngest daughter, Carola. Early next morning two detectives arrived, invaded our bedroom, collected his luggage and took it and him off to the Police Station. They had been on the landing stage in Liverpool, but had missed him in the fog. They went through all his belongings in his presence and let him go with everything except his passport and all his papers and notebooks. It amused us to think of the many dull hours they would have, going laboriously through a large number of sermons and lecture notes. After some time every single sheet of paper was returned intact, except Sir Cecil Spring-Rice's letter of withdrawal which, I suppose, lies still in some file of the C.I.D.

Leyton was now appointed General Secretary of the Fellowship of Reconciliation and immediately we all moved to London. Two aunts of mine lent us their house in Church End, Finchley, while they visited elsewhere. Their landlord, who lived next door, objected to a robust man of military age occupying the house. My aunts were most indignant and told him so, but we realized that they might lose their house on our account, so we lost no time in finding a furnished house for ourselves just opposite, with a different landlord. From an upstairs window in my aunts' house the children and I watched, with great interest and no full realization of its possible consequences, the first fleet of German zeppelins on its way to raid the centre of London.

I believe that Leyton was a thoroughly efficient Secretary of the Fellowship of Reconciliation, for in the office he was, as always, orderly and business-like, and in speaking up and down the country he had a wide outlook and experience and well-founded convictions on the peace question. At intervals the office was raided by the police and there were many signs that the Government would

have welcomed an opportunity of suppressing the organization for
" reconciliation " was at a discount. On one occasion when the
police appeared, Leyton said to them : " I will save you some trouble
by giving you straight away the most subversive literature we have
in this office " and handed them the New Testament. Though he
found happy association and comradeship within the F.O.R., he was
all the time longing to be back in the ministry of a Church where,
instead of speaking tours, always moving on to a new audience, he
would have a settled congregation and a chance of doing solid,
sustained teaching and building up of Church life. He met a
prominent Free Church minister in the train one day who said :
" Richards, you ought to be in a pulpit not in an office." " Yes,"
said Leyton, " I thoroughly agree with you, but will you give me a
Sunday in yours? " There was silence.

There were indeed very few Churches in the whole country
which would have risked having him in their pulpits for a Sunday.
Late in 1914 the Labour Leader had published a list of ministers
and clergy of all denominations who were known to be " anti-war "
and asked for information about others. Of course there must
have been many more, but on that list were only seven names,
including Leyton's. In a mood almost of despair in 1917, Leyton
wrote :

> If only the Churches would dare to be reckless and go and get
> crucified they might do something to save the world ; as it is they
> might as well be in their coffins. I suppose God Almighty can see
> the way out, but if I were in His place with my mortal vision I
> should snuff the Churches out and start afresh. He may do it yet,
> who knows! All the same, real Christianity is stronger than ever
> it was.

At last, in April 1918, a church in Liverpool, Pembroke Chapel,
belonging originally to the Baptists, invited Leyton to its pastorate.
It was a large down-town church whose most distinguished minister
many years earlier had been Augustine Birrell's father. It had
declined greatly since its palmy days under him, and its days of
popularity under Dr. Charles Aked, and had only a handful of
people left. Churches, I think, can be classified according to their
nature under various categories. Some are mere congregations,
some are fellowships, others communities ; and, in every Church
worth the name, there may be found a true communion of saints

most often among its obscure members. Pembroke Chapel was best described as a "band". "A band of hard-pressed folk are we" and yet "a happy band", fighting their way to a Jerusalem to be built among the dark, satanic mills of down-town Liverpool, fighting by way of agitation and demonstration. Shortly before we went there the members had walked in procession, headed by their minister, to the Council House to protest against what they felt to be some civic iniquity. They had the impression from what they had heard that Leyton, too, was an agitator, and so they invited him and he, longing to be back in a Church, accepted. They were disappointed in him.

The name "Pembroke Chapel" was mentioned in shocked tones in the more orthodox and conventional religious circles of Liverpool. The news that Leyton was going there had to be broken on one of her "good days", to an invalid aunt of mine, who was the widow of Charles Crosfield, one of Ian McLaren's elders in Sefton Park Presbyterian Church.

Most of the members of Pembroke were pacifists, but from a different standpoint from Leyton's. After several months one of the deacons conveyed to him that they were not accustomed to hearing so much about Jesus Christ and asked if he could introduce more reference to current political issues into his sermons and give the congregation a stronger lead on public questions? A comic change indeed!

The members were proud of their chapel and expected to work for it, and there was a fine gallantry about them. It was a great effort to the Church to raise Leyton's, by no means princely, salary, and, in addition, £40 towards our removal expenses which they had promised. So everybody put their shoulders to the wheel and just before Christmas there was a Christmas Fair which they asked me to open with Leyton taking the chair. His winter shirts were bought from one of the stalls, and never did he possess shirts so stout and hard wearing. The chapel was burnt to the ground a few years ago and I wonder what has happened to the happy band, and to the fowls which the caretaker kept on the premises and one of which Leyton met for the first time one Sunday morning roosting on the vestry mantlepiece.

When we had been in Liverpool a year, Leyton was invited to go back to Bowdon Downs. Never was he more astonished.

Whether to accept or not was a difficult decision to make. There had been such strain: would it recur or disappear? There had been such disunity on a fundamental issue: would a new unity be possible? Could he overcome his own self-consciousness whenever the war-peace issue again emerged? Could they overcome theirs? All these questions had to be faced. He could not fail to be impressed by the tolerance shown by such an invitation and, to him, tolerance against a background of deep conviction, always came high in the Christian virtues. When he had originally been asked to go to the Church the invitation had been unanimous. On this occasion eighty-four had voted for his return, ten had voted against, and the feelings of the latter deserved serious consideration. True, these ten, when they found the feeling of the majority, had withdrawn their adverse votes. One decisive factor, however, in Leyton's mind was that the three men sent to convey the invitation were all fathers of sons who had been fighting: one had lost a son, one had lost two. If *they* wanted him back Leyton felt it was a strong reason for going. Another reason for acceptance was that his leaving the Church in 1916 had been widely reported and commented upon and often misunderstood. Here was a way of showing outsiders, without words, that it was possible for a Church to keep the unity of Spirit in the bond of peace against great odds. So he said, "Yes."

We had gone through troublous times together in Bowdon Downs and had known one another, for better, for worse, below the surface, and it was on a deep level that the ministry was resumed.

The second Bowdon phase was entirely happy with a new possibility of permanent, constructive work, especially among the children and young people of the Church. There were memorable week-end conferences for young people, when a conference leader came from outside and religious problems were discussed and questions asked and answered. I well remember at one of these, Henry T. Hodgkin's able presentation of the evidence for the existence of God, and the impression made at another by George M. Ll. Davies as he presented the gospel of love and reconciliation as only he could.

For the children, a Guild was formed under the leadership of Miss Jessie Ostler with several able helpers, to which children came on their way home from school on Friday afternoons. Leyton always had tea with them and his arrival on the scene invariably created interest and merriment, for he could always entertain and excite children, though he did not find it so easy to get to know and understand them. The Guild members spent many months in making a large doll's house, complete in every detail, even to stair pads under the stair carpets and a piece of music on the piano. A real builder, who was a member of the Church, came and showed the boys how to tile the roof and glaze the windows. The children themselves chose to whom the house should be given and their choice fell on a boarding school for deaf children near Manchester. On the day of the presentation the deaf children came to tea and I still remember the look of gentle solicitude on the faces of some of the Guild children as they acted as hosts and hostesses.

There was an occasion, too, when they entertained Austrian children who were receiving hospitality in homes round Manchester, for a period of resuscitation after the deprivations and starvation of the war. A number of adult Church members came and looked on at the children of nations, recently kept apart by war, now playing happily together. We had one of the Austrian children as our guest for the night and well I remember how she went into peals of laughter when she saw our own three in their red dressing-gowns ready for bed. Pointing a finger at them, she choked out through gusts of laughter, " Bolsheviki! Bolsheviki! " There are many worse ways of dealing with ideological differences.

One Sunday morning, in the spring of 1923, Leyton came home to dinner saying, " Did you notice those three strange men sitting in church this morning? One of them I know—H. F. Keep of Carrs Lane, Birmingham. I know what that means, they are spying out the land." For Dr. Sidney M. Berry had just left Carrs Lane to become Secretary of the Congregational Union of England and Wales and the church was vacant. It is the custom in Congregationalism, when a church falls vacant, for the members to appoint a small selection committee, which arranges pulpit supplies and at the same time makes inquiries about a number of men and often visits their churches in order to get an impression of them against their accustomed background. It is only after these preliminaries that a man is invited to preach in the vacant church. The selection committee may consider a number of names but only one will be brought before the whole membership of the Church.

He may refuse or be passed over ; then the selection committee starts afresh : no two names are ever before a Church in competition with each other, and, apart from the Sunday when a " candidate " is in charge of the services, the pulpit is filled by men who are obviously not eligible for filling the vacancy. This, at any rate, is the procedure wherever the best Congregational tradition is observed. The final invitation is given only in the name of those in full membership of the Church.

This, then, was the procedure, the early stages of which Leyton detected as he saw the three men sitting in Bowdon Downs on that Sunday morning. Shortly afterwards he was asked to " take " a Sunday at Carrs Lane, which he refused. He was happy at Bowdon where we had many friends and he believed he was still doing useful work. In any case, he was sure that he lacked the popular gifts needed for a down-town city Church, with a congregation drawn from far-flung suburbs ; his preaching was too solid.

In June, however, he went to Oxford to attend, as usual, the Annual Council Meetings of Mansfield College, on which Mr. Keep and another Carrs Lane deacon also sat. Dr. Selbie, the Principal, took Leyton aside and gave him a thorough scolding for not even being willing to go and have a look at Carrs Lane. The invitation to preach there being renewed, he therefore accepted, much in the spirit of a fish being enticed into a net. He deliberately chose a sermon which would make plain his attitude on the war issue and hoped that would finish it. As he plunged through the door at the back of the church after the evening service, an elderly lady he already knew waylaid him with : " That was a dreadfully outspoken sermon you gave us this evening." " That's nothing ", he barked back at her, " to what I *can* do."

On his return home he felt no more inclination to accept if he were invited. " There was ", he said, " just a sea of faces. I couldn't even distinguish the features of those sitting at the back of the great gallery. I could never get to know them. And, of course, if I preached one of my peace sermons there during a war, that crowd would disappear like chaff before a wind." I am reminded of an incident related by Dr. Orchard—how he and his wife sat in a large building with crowds gathering to hear a well-known popular preacher : he murmured to her—" I could never fill a place like this." " No," she replied, " but you could empty it." And I am sure there was an admixture of pride in the witty remark.

Apparently, however, the crowd at the moment was prepared to swallow the strong meat and come back for more. In due course an invitation came with the backing of about six hundred members. Leyton still fought in his own mind against acceptance. He was no longer even faintly impressed by a crowd. Why should he be? He had preached a sermon to a crowded Free Church gathering in May 1914 and it had been received with plaudits and enthusiasm. He had repeated the same sermon, word for word, in a church in August 1914 and been asked not to preach there again. (And yet he never became a cynic, and kept a strong sweetness to the end because he was truly humble-minded and knew that others were faithful to Christianity where he failed.)

Back in Bowdon it was the staunch group of pacifists in the Fellowship of Reconciliation who felt most strongly he ought to go to Birmingham. To him it was a weariness to leave a Church where, as he put it, they "understand my idiom", and to have to start all over again in a Church with 1,200 members on its roll, where there had been only one man known to be a pacifist and conscientious objector in the 1914-18 war. There were, indeed, many pacifically minded people but there is a difference between a pacifist in time of war and pacifists in time of peace, like "vegetarians between meals", as Dr. Orchard once described them.

I had occasion to be in London for a few days at this time and it was as I sat in Kensington Gardens with the uniformed nurses pushing their prams past me and the children playing up and down, that it became clear to me that he ought to go to Birmingham. It was not easy to leave Bowdon, where we had so many friends, and the children had so much fun and companionship. It took Leyton longer to reach the same conclusion and, in the inner conflict and nervous tension of arriving at it, he lost his voice, as usual, which almost seemed to him a final justification for refusing! Once he had decided, he never had another doubt or regret, though he had some trepidation. In his last letter to the Bowdon Downs Church as its minister, Leyton wrote:

> This is not the place in which to review the reasons which induced me to accede to the call from Carrs Lane Church, Birmingham. I never had a more difficult decision to make; affection and the pull

of the work in Bowdon urged me to remain, but there was a still stronger pull in the sense of a call to a difficult work, and so I go.

It is difficult to say what I would in farewell; but there are some familiar words of John Robinson (the minister of the Leyden Church) to the Pilgrim Fathers, which are exactly apt to the situation, and for this purpose I make them my own:

"We were now ere long to part asunder," says one who was present, "and the Lord knew whether ever he would live to see their faces again. But whether the Lord had appointed it or not, he charged us before God and His blessed angels to follow him no farther than he followed Christ; and if God should reveal anything to us by any other instrument of His, to be as ready to receive it as ever we were to receive any truth by his ministry. For he was very confident that the Lord had yet more truth and light to break forth out of His Holy Word."

In that spirit he left Bowdon at the end of 1923 and entered on his new pastorate in February 1924.

Chapter XI

CARRS LANE, BIRMINGHAM—I

LEYTON RICHARDS WAS now, in 1924, in a Church which, since its foundation in 1748, had been known for its preaching, where the congregation assembled each Sunday with the expectation of hearing good sermons ; they were trained listeners. Once, in Oxford, I heard him thank the Rev. K. L. Parry of Bristol for a sermon, just delivered in Mansfield College Chapel : "That was great preaching, Parry," and Parry replied : "It takes great hearing to make great preaching," words which Leyton fully endorsed. He believed that at every service in a Free Church the sermon should lift up Christ before the people—"I, if I be lifted up will draw all men unto Me "—and that the speaking and the hearing should be a corporate act of worship.

An actor, or a musician, I imagine, finds that his art goes dead within him unless his audience lays itself open to any experience of beauty he has to offer. So it is with truth in preaching. Leyton used to say that while he was speaking he was conscious, without distinguishing a single face, of just the place in the congregation where there was a block of indifference or opposition ; conscious, too, of the exact moment when suddenly there was a withdrawal of acceptance of what he was saying. He had long since ceased to wish to "play on" an audience as he had been capable of doing, and to influence by rhetoric and eloquence. Once, years before, he had been suddenly and unexpectedly called on to address a large audience at a political meeting in Scotland, and the impression he made was thus recorded :

> We were under a cloud . . . things were going badly for us . . . the audience was rather tired of us and a little bored when he got up. In twenty minutes he was doing what he liked with them : they laughed, shouted, stamped as he desired, and when he said something about finishing, they yelled, "No, go on, go on."

He had enjoyed such experiences as much as any man but had deliberately put them behind him. He wanted to build up permanent, impregnable convictions, based on reason. This personally unambitious man did cherish some ambitions and one was to help to give the scientifically minded, the intellectually alert, the right to believe in Christianity. At the time of his death he was planning to spend the following winter in writing a book, of which the title would have been : " It stands to Reason ", in which he hoped to establish the fact that there need be no divorce between science and religion and that they need each other, and that " truth by whomsoever it is spoken comes from God ".*

If he distrusted the evanescent impression made by the mere exercise of popular gifts he distrusted equally the unreliable effect on the individual of being one of a great crowd. Soon after going to Carrs Lane he wrote in his annual letter to the members of the Church :

> Numbers are an entirely false criterion of the real life of the Church. . . . Even in apostolic and sub-apostolic days there were people who gloried in size and who boasted of their Churches that they were " rich and increased with goods and had need of nothing ". On the other hand, the ideal before any Church, be it large or small, is to be found in the tribute to the Church at Smyrna—" I know thy works and thy tribulation and thy poverty, but . . . be thou faithful unto death and I will give to thee a crown of life."

He did not ask, nor want, the full assent of his hearers to his own necessarily fallible and limited interpretation of Christianity, but he hoped to find in them as sincere and open-minded a search for Christian truth as he had himself brought to it : he had used his own faculties to their limit, he expected them to use theirs. One Scottish lady who attended Carrs Lane, used though she was to the strong meat of Presbyterian sermons, found that her usual light breakfast did not suffice on Sunday mornings ; she felt obliged to lay a foundation of bacon and egg to see her through! No member of a Church where he was minister ever found himself in a chapel of ease!

He had no wish to be surrounded by " Yes men " who sat at his feet and agreed with him. Once a man, who had just been nominated for the diaconate, came and asked if Leyton thought he ought to stand, seeing that he disagreed with him on many issues. The response was characteristic : it was to the effect that in a spiritual

* He had the Latin version of this sentence on his book-plate.

democracy, such as a Congregational Church professes to be, the decision should lie with the church meeting and that certainly he ought to let his name go forward if he was willing to serve.

I did not hear Leyton speak in public or preach till some time after we became engaged, so that I could never judge his preaching with detachment. He used to say that I was his severist critic and that he valued six words of praise from me more than sixty from most people. Nothing discouraged him more than to receive most praise for work with which he himself was least satisfied.

He used to come into Carrs Lane to conduct a service with a slightly bashful air and, as he came into full view of the congregation, half-way up the pulpit steps, he always turned his head away from them shyly. He had to work himself gradually into a feeling of ease and freedom, so always began by readings from the great devotional literature of other minds—Scripture sentences and liturgical prayers. He read the Bible well and enjoyed reading it, and by the time he came to the Old Testament lesson he was well into the spirit of the service. He always disapproved of the arrangement in some Free Churches, whereby a children's address had ousted one of the Scripture readings; he thought it a great come-down. By the time he reached the " long " prayer he gave to many members of the congregation—they have frequently testified—a sense of being in the conscious presence of God and of taking them there. His capacity for public prayer had developed with his own growth. In Bowdon days an old Presbyterian lady, who attended the church for the sake of his preaching, had said of him that she did wish he wouldn't wrangle with the Almighty in his prayers. When he reached the sermon it was difficult to remember that he had ever been shy or ill at ease : he was so completely master of himself and his material. He always ended by shutting the Bible with a bang and a quick Q.E.D. gesture. In an address given after his death, Dr. H. G. Wood said of his preaching, " He always made you feel you were a fool if you were not willing to be a fool for Christ's sake."

For more fundamental impressions of his preaching I must turn to others who may be presumed to be more objective than I can hope to be.

Shortly after his move to Birmingham, an article appeared in an American religious periodical,* introducing him to the religious

---

* *The Christian Century*, April 1925.

public across the Atlantic, signed "L.H.H.", an American, who knew Carrs Lane well. To him, therefore, I turn for my first description. He gave a full account of Leyton's chequered career and then went on :

> This courageous young man, who gave up his pulpit during the war, finds himself in one of the commanding ecclesiastical positions in the British Empire. You may be puzzled as you hear all this. But you are not perplexed after you have met the new minister of Carrs Lane. And especially you are not perplexed after you have heard him preach. He has the rare gift of a magnetic and compelling personality. But you soon go beyond this and sense certain qualities of soundness and sincerity which challenge your interest and command your respect. He is skilful in the give and take of speech, whether on the platform or in personal conversation. At a public meeting his replies to questions come with the quick impact of rapid fire and sure unhesitating aim. And all the while he gives you the sense of understanding his opponent, of apprehending his position, and of conceding everything which might be conceded. . . .
>
> Richards is fundamentally a thinker. And there is a certain massive quality about his thought which sometimes gives you a sudden sense of Dale himself. The process of his dialectic is clear, steady, and wide ranging. And this patient, firm onward movement without hesitation and without evasion or subterfuge gives you a fine sense of mental and moral satisfaction. . . .
>
> His use of English is noble, if not ornate, and there flashes forth a golden word from some bit of writing easily and happily, just because the word lives in his own mind and heart. Modern scholarship, history, and theology pay tribute in his sermons. He moves easily, but not without the authority of careful investigation and thoughtful meditation, among these baffling and manifold materials. There is passion in his preaching. But it is the passion of a mind kindled and glowing rather than the passion which is a substitute for thought. And with the almost rugged strength of his speech there is a sudden brightness and winsomeness. . . . Strength and beauty are both in his sanctuary. . . . There are men who speak to the mind. There are men who speak to the conscience. There are men who speak to the heart. It is a real prophet who speaks to all three together.

I must add a footnote here introducing the reality of shade as well as light. Not all felt, all the time, that Leyton was as understanding of his opponents as the writer of this article depicts him. He had his lapses and left some saying they would "have no more to do with that he-man". He could at times be merciless in debate even where his opponent was obviously of weaker mental calibre. He was once compared, on such an occasion, to "a terrier shaking the life out of a rat". One woman, now a pacifist, tells how she was held back from the pacifist position for a whole year by one such public debate. She had come as an open-minded inquirer and went away saying : "If this is pacifism in action it is not for me." But I think anyone who watched debates and controversies of his, either in the press or in public meetings over a long period, would feel that these were *lapses*. Some of his best friends were those whose opinions he had mercilessly sought to slaughter. On one occasion the Rev. George Shillito, with whom he was conducting a fierce public controversy, was actually staying under our own roof for the purpose of fuller discussion, and became a life-long friend, though both still held their own points of view. Leyton liked the people who stood up to him : he felt baffled and frustrated by those who, as one pacifist put it, "will neither accept our position nor meet our case".

There is another word I would add to L.H.H.'s description of him. Leyton himself always maintained that he was *not* "a great preacher", in spite of what, he knew, was said of him by some people. Only others could judge of that. Perhaps what he lacked was the element of poetry, which according to Dr. Johnson, "is the art of uniting pleasure to truth, by calling imagination to the help of reason". Certainly some missed this in him. On those occasions when "there flashed forth a golden word from some great bit of writing", a stillness fell on the whole congregation and they fixed their eyes upon him, like hungry people waiting for food. Browning put the case for the poetic presentation of truth when he wrote :

> But here's your fault ; grown men want thought, you think:
> . . . .
> Boys seek for images and melody,
> Men must have reason—so, you aim at men.
> Quite otherwise !

The poet comes and

> He with a "Look you ! " vents a brace of rhymes,
> And in these breaks the sudden rose herself,

Carrs Lane, Birmingham—I

Over us, under, round us every side

. . . .

Buries us with a glory, young once more,
Pouring heaven into this shut house of life.*

Yet Thomas Hardy showed, I believe, discerning shrewdness
when he wrote:

If Galileo had said in verse that the earth moved, the Inquisition
might have left him alone.†

Truth spoken in poetic language and unapplied, can be easily
dodged.

Would there have been any Crucifixion if it could have been said
of Christ to the end, "Without a parable spake He not unto
them"? And in spite of the perfection of the parables should we
have heard of Christ?

Let me add to the American's tribute, an Englishman's appreciation. In July 1925 "Martin Pew", of the *Christian World*, went
to hear Leyton preach in London and wrote an article from which
I quote some paragraphs:

What Carrs Lane thinks about a preacher to-day, England, or at
any rate, English Congregationalism—thinks about him to-morrow.
. . . He preached on Sunday at Grafton Square, Clapham, and I
was glad of the opportunity of trying to discover two things: why
Carrs Lane chose Mr. Richards and why Mr. Richards is so dead
certain that he is right on at least one fundamental problem of ethics.
Like some other active pacifists, Mr. Richards has, in Defoe's
phrase, "the lines of a soldier drawn in his face". I have seen a
well-known general with exactly the same type of profile. "Pugnacious" is not quite the word, but it is near enough. Add to this
a tall, upright figure, and a voice that could make a battalion "jump
to it" if necessary, though I have never heard on any parade ground
so musical a note. But I am sure that Carrs Lane chose Mr. Richards,
not because of his voice, but because of the things he says with it.
The things, not the words, . . . Judging from the sermon I heard,
Mr. Richards is showing his people how to look at religion from a
new angle, and showing them at the same time that it is the old
religion. If I wished to put things rather sensationally, I might
dwell on the fact that Mr. Richards went out of his way to defend

* Robert Browning: *Transcendentalism.*
† Thomas Hardy: *Diary. The Early Life of Thomas Hardy.*

the doctrine of the Trinity. Yet nothing could be more misleading. The argument of the sermon (on " what it means to be a Christian ") was that dogma and doctrine are hopelessly wrong angles from which to decide the question: Shall I be a Christian? You may end with dogma. Perhaps you may find such a dogma as the Holy Trinity the only adequate expression of your experience. But experience is the way in. The Christian experience begins with the historic fact of Jesus Christ. The second stage of the process is the discovery of the moral fact of Christ; the inescapable challenge of His life and teaching when the Man is honestly faced. In the third stage the moral fact becomes a spiritual fact—the conviction that God is only conceivable in terms of Jesus Christ. " God is what Jesus was." The dogma of the Divinity of Christ did not begin the dogma. The dogma arose inevitably out of our experience of Jesus Christ.

I could not help thinking of the contributed article in the *C.W.* last week in extenuation of the Fundamentalists' anxiety for an anchorage in " reality ". Mr. Richards took pains to show that there is no ground whatever for such anxiety so long as the eyes of the Church are fixed on the historic Jesus. Is that enough? If it is enough for one of the greatest Congregationalist Churches in the world, it means, surely, that Congregationalism is at the " quick march " in its advance to a position utterly different from Fundamentalism, or any " ism " born of anxiety.

The military phrase slipped in unasked. It reminds me of my curiosity as to how Mr. Richards became an uncompromising pacifist. Not, I think, because of any rigidly interpreted text. Nor, I suspect, because of any predisposition to general meekness. That he made his decision " honestly facing the historic Jesus " I do not doubt. . . . Mr. Richards, it is fair to surmise, has actually experienced the perilous adventure of peace; and it is the big risks and the chance of active service that have won him to enlist in that campaign. . . .

These military men, of course, have their weak side. They are very positive on some points about which we more timid people cannot help puzzling. While Mr. Richards is calling us to parade with that great confident voice of his, some of us may still be found wrestling with the problem of non-resistance, however fully we may share the great vision of a world at peace.

Most of that account could have been written by some one who had " sat under " Leyton Richards's ministry for a number of years, but one word at least would have been absent, the word " non-resistance ", for his mind had no place in it for " non-resistance ".

It was to no "non-resistant" passivity that he called men but to resistance in the spirit of Christ, not to *appeasement* but to *opposition* to evil which would not itself be a denial of the moral order of the Universe. He set forth his position fully in two books,* and it has been previously outlined. While pacifists are only a small minority in any nation they are almost entirely limited to a personal, individual witness; if they were to become a governing majority in any country Leyton believed that appropriate public action would be open to them. Constantly he was reading, studying, thinking, working out, how the moral law behind Christian pacifism could be expressed in practical politics, in economics, in diplomacy, in treaties, in international associations, and he worked with any group or society which seemed to him to be moving in the right direction, such as the League of Nations Union, Federal Union, and the National Peace Council; but he found in the Fellowship of Reconciliation and the Society of Friends the most nearly complete expression of his international ideals.

To return to Martin Pew and his assessment of Leyton Richards, he missed the mark when he associated him with non-resistance but as regards his attitude to fundamentalism, his assessment was right:

> Mr. Richards is showing his people how to look at religion from a new angle, and showing them at the same time that it is the old religion.

He always held that religion had nothing to fear from new scientific knowledge; and much to gain, from a careful, historical approach to the Bible, and a scholarly examination of its texts. From such an approach he himself found what seemed to him the fundamentals of the Christian faith even more firmly established, and I believe that it was because he made this plain that he encountered little opposition to his modern point of view. One Bowdon lady did indeed declare with some firmness that, despite all the evidence to the contrary, she would continue to believe that all the "Psalms of David" were written by him, as they could never mean the same to her if they were not. I cannot recall that Leyton ever came across anyone in any of his churches who avowed a literal belief in the Genesis account of Creation.

* *The Christian's Alternative to War.* Allen and Unwin. 1929.
  Christian Pacifism after Two World Wars. Independent Press. 1948.

When it came to the New Testament he was on more difficult ground. But whether he preached from texts in the Old or New Testament it was always clear that he acknowledged the Lordship of Christ in everything and that in Him was his standard of values. He made it plain, however, that acceptance of His Lordship did not depend on the miraculous elements in the Gospel narratives. For example, you might or might not believe in the literal stilling of the storm : that miracle was as nothing to Christ's power to subdue the storms and stresses in the souls of men and in society, once they were willing to take from His hands what they were ready to give. You might or might not believe in the Virgin Birth or a physical Resurrection, but you had not thereby affected your belief in His divinity or His continued presence with men. That depended on the divine quality of His life, and of His love, and of His death before which, if you faced it with single-mindedness, you bowed in reverence and awe. It was, to him, more important that you should arrive at the conviction that the nature of God is eternally like Christ than that you should begin at the other end with the doctrine of the Incarnation, though he believed you would eventually arrive there.

With regard to all Christ's miracles, however, he thought it wise not to underestimate what might be possible to a man utterly at one with the Will of God as was the Son of Man.

He was himself a Trinitarian though some misunderstood him sufficiently to doubt it. He saw in the Trinity the prototype of a perfect society existing at the very heart of the Universe, unity in diversity and diversity in unity, justifying man in his hope of, and striving towards, a perfect society among men.

More and more he dwelt on the fact that Christian principles cannot be fully carried out by individuals but must be embodied in a fellowship of persons. There were times when he had been tempted to despair of the Church, but, with all her sins and shortcomings, he saw no other society on earth even professing to base its corporate life on the principles of Jesus. He believed that within the Church these principles should be carried out without compromise and that, in certain matters, the Church should begin by setting her own house in order. This had various practical applications during his ministry at Carrs Lane which were initiated by, or acceptable to, the members. He believed, for instance, that the Church should be above reproach as an employer of labour and as an owner of house property. This issued in the appointment of an assistant caretaker so that one man, with heavy duties, should not work a seven-day week. The Church owned two or three small houses adjoining the caretaker's and all of these were reconditioned at considerable expense. He believed, too, that in an ideal world payment for work well done would be according to need and not according to " supply and demand ". It should not, therefore, be out of the question for an assistant junior colleague, to have the same or even a higher salary than his senior if his commitments and his needs were greater. It is a difficult principle to apply, for what are needs? But Carrs Lane has made an honest attempt to apply it. On two occasions Leyton applied for reductions in his own salary which, I am sure, would never have been suggested to him by the Church : first, at the time of the slump after the First World War, when many teachers and civil servants in Carrs Lane had reductions forced upon them ; second, when all three of our children's long years of education were over and they were beginning to earn instead of being an expense, and we felt his salary was more than we needed. It is a great responsibility to be paid entirely by the voluntary contributions of one's fellow members, many of them much poorer than their minister, and generous to the point of sacrifice. (But he was no sentimentalist about money. On another occasion, when he was Secretary of the Fellowship of Reconciliation in London in 1917, and our expenses were unavoidably heavy and beyond our means, he asked for a rise which was immediately and readily granted.)

Constantly he called the churches in which he ministered to be ready to become part of that great Invisible Church, the Body of Christ on earth, whose hands and feet and minds are at His service.

Chapter XII

CARRS LANE, BIRMINGHAM—II

THOUGH LEYTON REGARDED preaching as his first concern it was by
no means his only one. He was much immersed in public religious
work outside as well as inside Carrs Lane. For ten years he was
Chairman of the Free Church Extension Committee, which at the
time of his death thus recorded his contribution to church extension
in Birmingham :

> It was he, more than any other, who persuaded the denominations
> to set up an inter-denominational Church Extension Committee in
> order to meet the new situation arising out of the building of large
> housing estates on the outer ring of the City. . . . His statesman-
> ship helped to create confident and cordial co-operation, so that the
> various denominations were asked to work in the particular areas
> where they could best use the existing opportunities. Thus resources
> were wisely employed and all thought of competition was banished.

Added to this he persuaded various strong members of Carrs Lane
to leave the central Church and help build up the Church life in the
new areas, for he believed that each new Church should be helped
through its infancy by close contact with a well-established one.

It was not only with other Free Church denominations that Leyton
Richards had friendly association. He was also for a number of
years joint Chairman of the very active Christian Social Council of
Birmingham where Anglicans and Free Churchmen worked in
close and happy co-operation. At the time of his death, Bishop
Barnes wrote about him in *The Times* :

> Many of the differences which separate Christian communions
> became to him of little importance, and the co-operation of Carrs
> Lane with the Parish Church of Birmingham had a closeness without
> precedent in the ecclesiastical life of the city.

This was made possible by the Bishop's own encouragement of all
such co-operation, and also by Leyton's friendship with the Rector,
Canon Guy Rogers. He had moved far from the position he held

in his early days when a robust nonconforming spirit had been in evidence and he had faced Anglicans with a display of defensive equality, born of pride in our Free Church history and a tendency to patronize in some clergy. He had always held strongly that all the main branches of the Christian Church have some specific contribution to bring to the Church catholic and that each must guard its treasure till it has been safely deposited in the whole ; but that it is important to keep constantly in mind that others have treasures as precious and as much needed as one's own.

He was for several years Chairman of the Midlands B.B.C. Religious Broadcasts Committee. His own last broadcast in 1940 had a Christian pacifist emphasis. In the midst of war it was yet entirely uncensored but he was never asked to broadcast again.

His full programme meant that he overworked persistently year after year. The production of two sermons a week, when each was as carefully prepared and as full of concentrated matter as were his, was far too much. People used to say to him, " There was enough in this morning's sermon to make six." But he could no more thin them down than a barrister could cut out salient points in presenting a brief. He was often described as " Christ's advocate ", and he always, at work in his study, followed through in his mind the argument of the prosecution and was not satisfied unless he had met it point by point. He was incapable of doing a piece of slip-shod work and, when complaints reached him that his sermons made too great demands on his congregation's powers of concentration, he used to say : " After all there are many churches in Birmingham to which they can go for lighter fare, if that's what they want." His habit of mind, with his heavy correspondence, and the multitude of his inescapable public engagements, meant constant over-pressure. There would be a whole winter without one free evening. Sometimes there was hardly " leisure so much as to eat ". He would come into the dining-room in an abstracted kind of mood, hastily eat the first course, get up and say : " Let me know when the next course is in : I can't wait."

" In public or official affairs," writes Mr. Harold Nicolson, " the amount of work to be completed is always greater than the uninterrupted time available ; a state of anxiety is caused. . . . It is this time-pressure, more even than the sense of responsibility, which renders public, as distinct from private overwork so fearful an ordeal."* Thus he describes the overwork of public, highly placed officials. I do not suggest that the weight of Leyton's responsibilities was in any degree commensurate with those of a Minister of the Crown, but he did to some extent share the same sense of nervous tension and of always having much more to do than he had time for. He used to watch the time-table of great public servants, as recorded in the Press, with much sympathy. I tried to protect him from unnecessary interruptions as far as I could, sorting out the callers who ought to see him from those who needn't : always answering the telephone : interviewing the many beggars who found their way to our house, nearly all of them, in my experience, frauds —often very clever frauds, but terribly time-consuming. One caller (whose business made it quite legitimate to keep him out of the study, where I knew Leyton was finishing something promised to the Press for that day, under a great sense of pressure), as I showed him out, saying : " I have to act as his dragon," replied with a heavy scowl, " I see you do." Leyton used to be irritated by the fact that a minister is supposed to be available for callers without appointment, at any time, on any kind of business, whereas no one expects his doctor or his solicitor to be. His unwillingness to be diverted from what he conceived to be his main tasks was a strength but it was also, at times, a weakness. He showed deep sympathy with individuals within the limits of his imagination, which is the most which is within the scope of anyone. But his imagination would have been enlarged if his time-table had allowed more frequent personal contacts and more patient listening. No man can do everything and he was inclined to believe a group of Churches might combine in using the services of several men, one mainly concentrating on pulpit work, one on pastoral care, another on the education of youth, according to their several aptitudes, and he knew that few men are adequately equipped for all three.

If the Church officers had not recognized that his duties imposed too heavy a burden he could not have got through. They were generous in the steps they took to give relief. Almost every three years he was liberated to go to the U.S.A. or Canada for lecturing and preaching tours—strenuous, but a great relief from the constant preparation of fresh material. At the end of ten years, in 1934, he was granted a Sabbatical year which he spent, partly across the

---

* *The Spectator*, March 4th, 1949.

Atlantic, partly in the theological colleges of this country. By a very happy arrangement, the well-known Presbyterian minister, Dr. Herbert Gray, took charge of Carrs Lane and made countless friends in the Church and in Birmingham, and continued after Leyton's return to take charge one Sunday in every month. It was a highly successful colleagueship.

Leyton's time-table left little room in it for any detailed attention to the Christian nurture of children and young people in Carrs Lane. Parents, wrestling with the manifold problems of bringing up their families, felt that they needed more help and expert guidance than he was able to give. The diaconate and Church Meeting also decided that the several Sunday Schools and young people's organizations needed trained leadership. Therefore, in 1928, the Rev. Dorothy Wilson was appointed to be in charge of work among young people. She was followed after an interval, in 1933, by Mr. Godfrey Pain, whose genius created a young people's organization known as the Seventy Club. Finally, in 1938, the Rev. Alan G. Knott was appointed as Joint Minister, and became not only a colleague but a friend.

Leyton never regarded his ministry anywhere in terms of pacifist propaganda, but as the building up of the faith of the Christian believer, and the advocacy of Christianity to the inquirer. But as, to him, one of the implications of Christianity was a repudiation of war, it was not surprising that gradually there grew up in Carrs Lane a number of convinced pacifists. When he had been there for nearly ten years, in the autumn of 1933, these expressed their strong wish to form themselves into a visible fellowship, to be known as the Carrs Lane Pacifist Group, and to be affiliated with the Fellowship of Reconciliation.

The *Christian World* of February 1934 reported that 286 members of Carrs Lane Church had signified their agreement with the Christian pacifist position and this number increased later on to over 300. About forty members of this group felt a " concern " to share their conviction on Christianity and War with others. They read and studied and discussed for several months and then, in 1934, sent out letters to many Churches and societies of all denominations, first in Birmingham, then farther afield, asking if they might send speakers to present the case for Christian pacifism. They received many hundreds of invitations, mostly to small groups, and spoke at meetings over a period of five-and-a-half years. Almost all the men and women involved had full-time jobs, so that this work was done after working hours and at their own expense. Usually two or three went together : it was always the aim to have one ex-service man and one woman in the "team", and to leave literature behind them and lists of books for study. They began their work in Birmingham, and then went as far afield as Coventry, Lichfield, Nottingham, London, and all through the Potteries. One man, who had to travel on business, spoke in places in North Wales and was instrumental in starting an F.O.R. group in Chester.

Views as to the desirability of much of the peace and pacifist propaganda during the two World Wars are sharply divided. I can testify, at any rate, as the wife of a "notorious" pacifist throughout them both, to the immeasurable difference in general atmosphere between the two. By 1939 many illusions as to the limits of what war can accomplish had gone. A young relation said to us : "We shall fight and we shall die, but we shall no longer believe in it as they did in 1914, when they actually thought it was a war to end war." Pacifism in 1914-18 was an almost new term,* little known and still less understood outside the Society of Friends, and pacifists had to be constantly on the defensive. In the Second World War, on the other hand, the *Church* had begun to be on the defensive. In 1930 the Bishops had declared that "war as a method of settling international disputes is contrary to the teaching and example of our Lord Jesus Christ" and had found it necessary later, always with one dissentient voice, to explain why, nevertheless, they considered it legitimate for Christians to engage in it. Phrases had become current in religious circles such as "an impossible perfectionism" and "the lesser of two evils". Pacifists, too, had thought through their position more thoroughly. Thousands of mostly unknown conscientious objectors were "obstinate" in the First World War, and many hundreds of mostly nameless pacifists testified to their faith between the wars, and Quakers continued their peaceful penetration. Without them would Mr. Winston Churchill have written a certain passage in his first volume of the history of the Second World War?

---

* The words "pacifist", "pacifism", do not appear in the large Oxford Dictionary, published 1909, but first in the 1933 Supplement. The rise of a word betokens the rise of an idea.

Those whose inclination is to bow their heads, to seek patiently and faithfully for peaceful compromise are not always wrong. On the contrary, in the majority of instances they may be right, not only morally but from a practical stand-point. How many wars have been averted by patient and persistent goodwill! Religion and virtue alike lend their sanctions to meekness and humility, not only between men but between nations. . . . The Sermon on the Mount is the last word in Christian ethics. Everyone respects the Quakers. Still it is not on those terms that Ministers assume their responsibilities of guiding States.*

Truly, pacifism is in the air, even though many may be inclined to think it pollutes it! And pacifists still go on hoping and praying that some day Statesmen *will* assume their responsibilities on the basis of the Sermon on the Mount, for we believe it to be not only good religion but practical good sense.

At Carrs Lane, though there was still a large number of members who did not accept the pacifist position, the Pacifist Group was formed and its work undertaken with the knowledge and consent of the Church Meeting. It was not easy for the non-pacifists, for outsiders began to speak with distaste of Carrs Lane as a " pacifist church ". They often found themselves explaining that their minister stood for something wider than pacifism—Christianity which included the tolerance towards others he claimed for himself.

The whole Church, however, could unite in a keen interest in international affairs other than pacifism. Though they worked in and for their city in various ways, their concern went far beyond Birmingham, or their own denomination. Carrs Lane has always been a missionary Church and has had many men and women abroad in missionary work. In addition, year after year, during Leyton's ministry, members worked and made and mended, and collected for Coalfields Distress Fund, for Chinese Relief, for Spanish Relief, and later for various refugee funds. The Peace Ballot in Birmingham was organized by Mr. T. N. Veitch, a deacon of the Church, and proportionately more votes were polled here than in any other city. Later Mr. H. W. Gosling, another deacon, had a large part in the founding and in the running of the International Centre which is now a permanent institution in the life of Birmingham. During the persecution of the Jews in Germany, Carrs Lane made a gesture of sympathy to members of the Jewish communion

* *The Gathering Storm*, Vol. 1, pp. 250-51.

in Birmingham when Dr. Cohen, the Chief Rabbi, and Leyton, conducted a joint service in the church. There was much friendliness between Jews and Christians in Birmingham, in which Canon Rogers at the Parish Church played a leading role.

At the end of 1936, being convinced that a change of ministry would be for the good of the Church, Leyton sent in his resignation. "Every man's presentation of the Gospel", he wrote, "is subject to the limitations of his personality, and the Gospel is too many-sided to find adequate expression, over a long period, through the lips of one man." Before he went to Carrs Lane, I well remember being present when he told Mr. H. F. Keep, a deacon who came as an emissary to see him, that he anticipated a period of seven years as the longest likely to be fruitful and now he had exceeded this by nearly six. He realized that his presentation of his faith was so definite and clear-cut that it could soon be grasped, and the general outline of what he was likely to say would soon be anticipated. By 1936 there had been a marked decline in the size of the congregation ; the large core of Church members, and regular attenders, were faithful and active, but the floating, church-going population had wandered elsewhere or nowhere. Leyton did not set any great value on mere numbers, yet he believed that one of the justifications for having a church building placed, as Carrs Lane was, far from residential districts, in the midst of warehouses and shops, with the clang and grind of trams and buses going by, was to serve the unattached seeker after religious conviction. He himself hated going into the centre of a city for Sunday worship and travelling by bus or tram : for many years he bicycled the four miles to and from the suburb where we lived.

Though he felt he ought to resign, it was a costly decision to make, for he was deeply attached to the Church and supremely happy in it. Indeed, on the day his letter of resignation, which had been drafted and re-drafted, was at last in its final form, he could not bring himself to post it, and, in the evening, went and talked the matter over, not for the first time, with Mr. Keep, a man whose sagacity he respected. He got back from Edgbaston two hours later, seeming happy and relieved, with the letter safely in the pillar box. The matter, however, was not settled yet and a period of strain and indecision followed, for, while a number of Church members and officers welcomed his resignation, a larger number strongly urged him to withdraw it. Outside influences, too, were brought to bear on both sides—some friends urging him to leave in order to be free for wider work (his correspondents at this time, both from at home and abroad, had reached overwhelming numbers). Others represented to him the importance, now that war clouds were gathering, of having in a leading Free Church pulpit a man who had for years concentrated attention on international affairs. Some friends, including non-pacifists, pointed out that, should war come, it would be in itself a public demonstration that freedom of conscience, and liberty of speech were being upheld in Britain to have a pacifist in a position where he could hardly be overlooked.

My own view—possibly a self-interested one—was that he should stick to his decision to resign, which he had not made lightly. I knew that wherever he had been in charge of a Church, Leyton had left behind him a definite point of view, had created it for some minds, and at least introduced an awareness of it in all who listened to him with any regularity. Even the three brief years in Melbourne had "branded" many with it for life, as they still testify. And it seemed to me that in a ministry which concentrated on teaching and preaching, rather than on the pastoral office or on organization, it was its quality which counted rather than its length. I believed that leadership, which is real and lasting, can after a time be, to advantage, dispensed with. I knew that his voice, though silent in Carrs Lane would be heard elsewhere. Professor Ernest Barker wrote about British Statesmen:

> It is easy to exaggerate the influence of a single personality in the field of constructive creation. The series matters more than any part or person in the series.*

This seems to me to apply to "constructive creation" in ministers of religion as well as in ministers of the Crown. I hoped that those who greatly valued his sermons took into account the cost in terms of his own health and nervous tension, and in the foregoing of many worthwhile contacts and opportunities. He was too modest himself to give due weight to these as determining factors. Though the Carrs Lane diaconate had given most generous recognition to his particular physical and mental make-up and had eased the burden in every possible way, he seemed to me to have carried the duties of

---

* *British Statesmen.* "Britain in Pictures" Series.

a city Church long enough. Like other wives, however, in similar circumstances, when I realized fully how relieved some people in Birmingham and even in Carrs Lane itself were at the thought of his leaving, especially because he was a pacifist, my feelings became unduly complicated and "contrary"!

Leyton himself was in a strait betwixt two, and only anxious to do the right thing. Believing, as he always did, in the spiritual capacity of the Church Meeting to arrive at right judgments, he put himself in their hands and a Meeting was held on January 26th, 1937, which was thus reported at the time:

> The feeling abroad in the Meeting was not concerned with what any particular group of persons wished or what Mr. Richards himself might personally desire, but rather what was God's will for him and the Church in the work of His Kingdom: should it be continued in Birmingham or carried on elsewhere? . . . A distinct and over-whelming feeling was indicated that Mr. Richards was needed not only for the work of Carrs Lane itself but for its wider ministry to the City of Birmingham. . . . The Chairman, Mr. H. W. Gosling, reported to him that speaking for the Meeting as a whole, the Church confirmed his charge and pledged itself to renewed efforts to over-come any deficiencies there might be in the fellowship and to rededicate themselves as Church members under his leadership.

And so began another phase in his Carrs Lane ministry. He had received other than a mere "vote of confidence", he had been given a new commission and a renewed pledge of co-operation in carrying it out. The meeting which had originally invited him to Birming-ham had numbered about six hundred; the meeting which asked him to remain numbered less than half, but it knew more surely what was involved.

This portrait often seems to get out of focus and Leyton appears as a grim prophet, carrying the weight of the world's international problems on his shoulders. Only those who knew him at a distance could think that. I always rather shrank from speaking to strangers after Carrs Lane services which seems to be one of the duties expected of a minister's wife. One Sunday an unknown lady was pointed out to me as having been coming regularly on Sundays for many weeks and sitting near me, who ought to be "welcomed in". So, against my own inclination, and indeed on this occasion against my better judgment, I accosted her after the morning service, asked her if she knew anybody, or would care to be introduced to the minister. She solemnly replied : " I have never met Mr. Richards and I hope I never shall. I come to hear him preach but I have come from a suburban Church to get away from all that." I trust she didn't mind, but I shook her warmly by the hand and felt justified in accosting no more strangers for a good many weeks. Fortunately, many were glad to get a nearer view of the minister and they found him full of fun and jollity, with an endless stream of apt anecdotes, enjoying good company and good talk. He was a member of the Rotary Club and much enjoyed the Monday lunches, which he never missed if he could help it. It is said that on one Monday the speaker's subject was British railways, on which he was an authority : at question time he was asked a question he could not answer, but Leyton could and for the rest of the session all the questions were fired at him and he was able to supply the answers. The Rotary story, however, had an unhappy ending. When Leyton finally left Carrs Lane and therefore lost the qualifying category necessary for membership, the Club made him an honorary life member, an honour seldom bestowed, which pleased him very much. When the 1939 war came and he was still a pacifist, he was told unofficially that the honour no longer represented the feeling of the Club, so he quietly resigned, with disappointment, but entirely without resentment, for he understood.

Through all these years throat trouble dogged him, and became unmanageable in 1938, so that, at the end of that year, he felt it necessary to resign from Carrs Lane, after being told by a specialist that irreparable damage had been done, which no treatment could cure. However, the Church, generous as always, asked him to remain as their minister for a further six months without any pulpit duties. He was never one to take anything lying down, and he still persisted in searching for a cure for his throat trouble and, during the early months of 1939, came across a new system of voice production which was a great help. He had in the meantime left Carrs Lane and accepted a Fellowship at the Quaker College, Woodbrooke, on the outskirts of Birmingham. When war broke out Carrs Lane had still not filled his place and the following paragraph from *The History of Carrs Lane* records what happened :

Perhaps the finest tribute to Richards's ministry is to be found in the record of that ever-dreadful September 1939. He had commenced his new work and a Selection Committee had begun the search for a successor, when he received a telephone call from the senior officers of the Church (who were not pacifists) asking him to come back and preside at the forthcoming Church Meeting and "to steady us". Not only did he perform that memorable task, but he helped the Church for two years by conducting the Sunday services.

Chapter XIII

AMERICA AND CANADA

LEYTON WAS ALWAYS looking forward to his "next trip across the Atlantic"; all through the Second World War he was longing for the time when he could make another visit to add to his fourteen, but when it became possible it was no longer, for health reasons, practicable. I went with him four times and once Margaret was with us.

He looked upon the U.S.A. as his second homeland, he knew its history in detail, and always had a portrait of Abraham Lincoln hanging on his study walls. He revered the American Constitution and saw it as the best contemporary example of the federal principle to which he hoped and believed the whole world would ultimately move forward, where local and historical differences and loyalties would be preserved, but where there would be a fusion of the citizens in a still wider allegiance. The plain, unadorned opening words of the preamble to the Constitution: "We, the people of the United States", and the inscription on the silver dollar, *e omnibus unum*, expressed to him great conceptions of nationhood, already partly realized. However materialistic were some contemporary manifestations of American power, he never ceased to believe in another kind of American greatness, spiritual in its nature, generous, freedom-loving and idealistic. He saw the people of the U.S.A. destined to make a unique contribution to the life of the world, using their vast material resources, not to dominate but to serve mankind. Nothing could ever shake this confidence, and any adverse critic always found him springing to the defence of America.

Moreover, he maintained that Americans are humble-minded, and that in any case you do not get a fair picture of any people away from their home background. (How ashamed we once were of an English party, in a Swiss train, where they behaved as though Switzerland belonged to them!) A newspaper man, interviewing him in 1925, after an American visit, confessed that he was dumbfounded by Leyton's response to his opening gambit which had been,

" Well, I suppose our friends over there are still talking very loud ? " ;
to which the reply was : " I find them extraordinarily humble,
teachable and conscious of their own limitations," and the interview
ended by his saying :

> There is a fine incalculable element over there, a sort of moral
> drive which makes me exceedingly hopeful. Perhaps it is due to
> their Puritan inheritance, but when once a disposition becomes a
> conviction America acts. . . . How soon America will catch fire
> on internationalism I cannot say. It may be two years, it may be
> ten. But America, I am convinced, cannot permanently remain
> outside our present-day movements for securing peace.

He marvelled at their extraordinary capacity for absorbing alien
elements. In a High School he visited he found the words,
" Americans All ", carved in the wall above the table which held
the school register. There were 1,500 pupils, of whom 943 were of
non-American parentage, and the list began with Abbatt and ended
with Zoschiczha. He felt that the difficult achievement of bringing
those children to a state of mind where they could say, " We, the
people of the United States," and be called " Americans All ", was
too little appreciated in Britain, and he explained certain crude and
sensational features of contemporary American life as due to the
necessity for appealing to a large, cosmopolitan population spread
over a vast area.

A European refugee in Britain during the Second World War
said to me : " Here in England you are very polite to us, very kind,
and you take endless trouble on our behalf ; but we do not feel we
are really wanted, or that we shall ever get to know you." A
generalization not fully warranted, but it illustrates a difference.

Leyton found Americans, young and old, apparently at ease in
most situations. Sometimes their sense of freedom and their self-
confidence expressed itself in ways which seem a little odd to a
Britisher but, on the whole, he felt they were fortunate in being
liberated from many crippling, conscious and sub-conscious tensions.
He smiled both inwardly and outwardly when a little nine-year-old
girl, who had joined the procession which always greets a visiting
preacher after a service, congratulated him on " that mighty fine
sermon ". American children did, at times, take one's breath
away but we agreed with the old American professor who remarked
that he often wondered how it was that " such insufferable youngsters

LEYTON RICHARDS OFF DUTY

[facing page 100

as our children frequently are apt to be, grow up into such mighty fine men and women ".

On his many visits Leyton came in contact with all sorts and conditions of men. He spent his railroad journeys mostly in the Parlour Car talking to anyone who would talk to him : he preached in churches of various denominations ; he worked with Friends ; he addressed, I suppose, thousands of meetings with audiences which included Episcopal and Presbyterian, and Labour Leaders' Summer Schools, Institutes on International Relations, High Schools, Colleges and innumerable luncheon clubs. He had one particularly exacting speaking tour, arranged by the National Council for the Prevention of War, with meetings beginning with public breakfasts and ending late at night. He could not be blind to the defects in the American scene. He felt for himself the attempted pressure by Big Business to control freedom of thought in church and university, when just before conducting the service in a famous church, one of the officers said to him in the vestry : "We hope very much, Mr. Richards, that you are a middle-of-the-road man." Doubtless within the next hour they were able to find out! He had a taste of the vulgarity possible in certain circles when he discovered on one occasion, just before preaching, that time-on-the-air for broadcasting his sermon had been bought by a promise that in return a certain Lumber Company would be mentioned three times during the service. He found too much " creaturely activity ", to his own way of thinking, in the elaborate organization and manifold busy-ness of many Churches, and in the too prominent machinery of their ways of worship. "They vie with the world ", he wrote in his diary, " in the terrific pace and variety of life : but need they ? A quiet intensive ministry would be an experiment worth trying. I believe folk would turn to it as the thirsty to water. Processionals and recessionals, robed choirs, responsive readings, order and ceremonial, are no substitute for the spirit of worship ; but the danger in America would seem to lie in that direction : and the minister becomes a kind of stage director or actor-manager." This entry was written after a particular experience of one type of American Church ; but he often found what he wanted, especially in small country towns, where the simple, beautiful Colonial architecture of the buildings, in itself, suggested reverence and dignity and peace.

No picture of American life is complete which misses out the negro

8

and the negro problem. The sense of unity among white people is far from being shared by them and Americans are not being allowed to forget it by critical outsiders, nor do the best of them wish to. The general position is so well known that I need not dwell on it nor on Leyton's reaction to it, but will only relate various small incidents which we saw for ourselves when in contact with negroes; we met them both in the North and in the South, in many walks of life and on many occasions.

At Duke University in North Carolina we watched Southern negro domestic labour at work : a troop of women came in each morning to clean the college rooms and corridors : they leant on their broom handles and chatted and laughed with each other and sometimes remembered to get down to a little cleaning. It is said that part of the negroes' equipment for taking his place in the modern world, with its ever-decreasing working hours, is his capacity for enjoying leisure in inexpensive ways! He can be happy, down south, for hours on end, in a rocking chair on his front porch, watching the world go by.

But what we saw in North Carolina does not give a fair picture of negro labour in general, which can rise to high standards of industry and efficiency. A negro servant in Philadelphia insisted on re-washing a whole sink-full of crockery because her mistress had rinsed her hands over it! In Washington we visited an apartment where there was a ninety-year-old servant who had actually been born in slavery. She was quite illiterate and almost without power of speech, but she served her old mistress with entire devotion. During an illness of the latter she refused to go home at nights to the negro quarter where she lived, but stretched herself out on the bare floor across her mistress's bedroom door until the illness was over. She had the eyes of a faithful old dog.

On two occasions we went into negro churches. In Atlanta, Georgia, where we wanted to have conversation with a negro who had been trained at Mansfield College, Oxford, there was not a hotel or a restaurant of either race which would admit the other, for there is racial pride on both sides of the colour bar. But we did ask permission, through him, to attend a Sunday service in the negro Methodist church. There was reverence and reality there, and, at the same time, an informality strange to us. There were two collections during the service and these were taken up by little girls, with their crinkly black hair tied up with bright ribbons, to whom the people chatted pleasantly as they moved up and down the aisles. The singing was beautiful: the slim black girl at the organ swayed slightly as she played and improvised elaborate syncopations which were taken up by the choir and the congregation, and still further elaborated. During the service they sang two spirituals, "Steal away to Jesus" and "Go down Pharaoh", and I can well understand why negroes resent their sorrow-songs being sung in drawing-rooms and on concert platforms, by white people, for the entertainment of white people.

The other church occasion was of a different order. We were taken by friends to a concert in a Haarlem church, in aid of a fund for negro Boy Scouts. While a world-famous violinist was playing, a black steward, with self-importance and insouciance, was collecting hymn-books in the back gallery just above his head, a provision for the singing of a closing hymn which had evidently been overlooked. Higher and higher got the pile of books precariously balanced against his chest as he moved to and fro, and we held our breath waiting for it to descend at any moment on the head of the unconscious violinist.

Negroes in Georgia told us how they had been asked to take part in a Methodist Church Pageant of the Lives of the Wesleys, which included episodes in which members of their race appeared. They rehearsed their part under the producer, but when they got to the public hall for the performance they found they were to be admitted to the building only through the service door where heavy goods were unloaded. Rather than spoil the whole pageant they swallowed their pride, but it took a deal of swallowing.

A famous negro choir came across to give concerts in Europe: they sang before the King and Queen and were made much of. One of the last engagements of their leading quartette was to sing in Carrs Lane Church and they came home with us afterwards. We asked them what they had enjoyed most in their tour. They said, without the slightest hesitation, that it had been riding on the front of a charabanc on a sight-seeing trip round London with South Africans *sitting behind them*; that the South Africans had made a row at the booking office when they found negroes in the front seat, and demanded their money back, but the booking clerk had told them: "First come, first served in England: if you don't like the seats you needn't go, but there's no reason to give your money back to you." That indeed was something for our friends to write home about!

We met a number of well-educated, cultured negroes both North and South. On a charabanc journey to the Grand Canyon a large limousine travelled beside us, occupied by one bland-looking negro in clerical dress. He had booked an ordinary seat but two smartly-dressed New York women had objected to travelling in the same vehicle, so the company, who had not been aware of his colour when he booked by mail, had to provide a separate car. We talked to him at our various halts and found that he had received his university education at Magdalen College, Oxford. He asked Leyton next time he was in Oxford to give his greetings to the President of his old college.

Up in the North we talked to a negro lady who said that she and her husband would have liked to identify themselves more closely with their own race, by moving South and taking part in educational and social work there, but they had a daughter and dare not go South for fear of the "White Peril".

The despair of many negroes is the apathy of their own race and their failure even to take advantage of the opportunities already open to them. Some said to us that many of those who are alive to the unjust discrimination against them, believe they have been meek and patient too long and must learn to be aggressive and pugnacious like the white man, and to fight for their rights.

The best of both races are much exercised in mind over the problem, alive to its manifold difficulties, and determined to work *together* for a solution.

We, in this country, have no reason to feel superior. The average Englishman transplanted to South Africa, where he meets negroes in vast numbers, behaves in much the same way as the average American. And in Georgia they told us, "You, in England, are willing to be entertained by us, but you don't regard us as equals. The Mills Brothers, with the wife of one of them, traipsed about London for twenty-four hours before they could get anyone to give them any sort of accommodation."

* * * *

And now to pass on to Canada. There is an archway in the State of Washington where the two countries meet, which bears an inscription on the American side : " May these Gates never be closed. Children of a Common Mother " ; and on the Canadian side : " Brethren Dwelling together in Unity." That there should ever be war between them is quite unthinkable. It is possible to have a foot in each country at one and the same time, and yet the difference in atmosphere is immediately felt. Travellers often make a gradual approach to Canada up the wide reaches of the St. Lawrence, whereas America presents itself with dramatic suddenness in the sky-line of New York. Something of the same feeling persists throughout a visit. In both countries we are in the New World, but the transition between new and old is much less abrupt in Canada. She never forgets her roots whether they be British or French ; she is a child asserting her independence indeed, but always as a member of the family, and with some feeling of kinship with " the old folk at home ".

Leyton travelled right across Canada several times, lecturing and speaking and preaching, and in 1928 he exchanged pulpits for three months with Dr. Richard Roberts of Toronto, who had preceded him as Secretary of the British Fellowship of Reconciliation. His diary of those summer months records various impressions :

> A sense of buoyancy and hope characterises Canada—despite seasonal unemployment and other difficulties. There is land everywhere and men have the sense that if they fail in one place they can move elsewhere and start afresh. This is often an illusion. . . . The atmosphere is exhilarating, spiritually as well as physically. But it is the exhilaration of the Garden of Eden rather than of the City of God, for it comes *not* of solving problems but of the absence of problems. . . . Wealth here is seemingly entirely unburdened by an uneasy conscience for the poor ; for poverty and slums do not exist in the English sense, and the sense of opportunity and hope which abounds makes wealth seem a possibility for every one. . . . Had a gorgeous three days in cloudless sunshine and forest-scented air. Visited a musk-rat farm, and the government forest fire control station. Saw woodchucks, a log jamb in a creek, swallow-tail butterflies, two bootleggers convicted of distilling whisky, on the way to jail, beaver dams, and numbers of lakes, falls and rivers. Went through the Long Swamp on a corduroy road and talked with lumbermen and trappers—all most interesting.

In this year, 1928, he found the Canadian Church hopeful and enthusiastic because of the consummation of the union of Methodism,

Presbyterianism and Congregationalism in the United Church of Canada three years earlier. He records a remark of Dr. Moffatt's that those opposing church union "always seemed to have suffered spiritually in consequence". He spent much time in observing the results and in asking innumerable questions, and he was most favourably impressed. He was satisfied that Congregationalism had brought its specific contribution to the whole and had preserved its spiritual liberty. He wrote at the time:

> The major sacrifices in the cause of union have been made by the former Methodist Church in Canada. All three denominations of course yielded something, but, so far as I can judge, the Methodists most of all and yet they did it with absolute unanimity and with a grace and enthusiasm which were a true earnest of their Christian spirit. This, it seems to me, is bound to have had its reaction upon the life of the Church, for it is a spiritual law which applies to groups as to individuals that we get as we give!*
>
> The advantages, both temporal and spiritual, of union are so obvious and splendid [as to offset completely] the minor irritations and misfits which inevitably accompany a fusion of interests. The chief gain is the release for the service of the Kingship of God of countless energies previously devoted to denominational maintenance and sectarian rivalry. . . . That is not to say that the United Church is able to make a full-orbed witness: that cannot be until other elements are also incorporated.†

In a lecture on the subject of Canada, Leyton gave it as his judgment that, though technically, because of her population, a "Little Nation", she has great significance *for* though not *in* world affairs. First, strategically, she is the centre of air communications in the Northern hemisphere. But, more important, politically, she has solved problems which still vex the rest of the world for she has achieved political unity, despite geographical difficulties and economic and cultural differences; and she has maintained independence within a wider imperial system. She shows political wisdom and maturity for she has established peace between her several provinces, and with her powerful next door neighbour, by law and not by armed defence.

---

* *Sherborne Church Magazine.*   † *The Christian World.*

Chapter XIV

IN JOURNEYINGS OFT

IT WAS ALWAYS more difficult to go to Europe than to America or Canada because there was no way of earning fees to foot the bill. In spite of that we managed it a number of times. It was always possible to stay in cheap hotels or hostels, and to travel in the cheapest class, and by the least expensive routes. There were times, however, when we enjoyed travelling in real comfort owing to the kind generosity of a Birmingham travel agent, the late Mr. J. Johnson, a member of Carrs Lane, known to his many friends as " J.J."

Two of our daughters went abroad for some months between school and college to add fluency to school French and their sojourn in each case was rounded off with a family holiday. One summer we all went to a small hotel in the mountains of the Black Forest where only one English guest had ever stayed before. Leyton was wearing a college blazer complete with crest, and when we got to know our fellow guests we found that they had supposed he was a British admiral!

Some of our European visits, sometimes with one or more of our children, combined holiday-making with more definite fact-finding projects. On four occasions Leyton and I timed a summer holiday to end at Geneva while the Assembly of the League of Nations was in session and one year he acted as correspondent there for the *Birmingham Post*. It is melancholy reading to look through notes and diaries of these visits and to remember afresh what a wonderful instrument the League might have been in hands determined to use it. In its early days delegates were sent representing the whole nation—men who took a world view and were great humanitarians like Nansen, Cecil, Gilbert Murray, Count Apponyi. These were succeeded by Foreign Secretaries, representing the policy of their several Governments. So often these officials seemed to engage in diplomatic manœuvring, in contrast to the broad planning of their predecessors who had a world outlook.

For example, in 1932 the British Delegation initiated a discussion on the cutting down of the expenditure on the League which prolonged the Assembly for a whole week : thereby they spent more than they set out to save, and, in any case, how many minutes, or seconds, of the Second World War's expenditure did the whole annual cost of the League represent to each nation?   Yet various nations were always in arrears.

We were present on various historic occasions, which might have been turning points in the history of the League.   In 1934, when Russia was admitted, we heard Litvinoff, on behalf of the U.S.S.R., pledge his country to observation of every part of the Covenant.   He added, " The Soviet Government is especially glad to be coming into the League at a moment when the question of the amendment of the Covenant in order to bring it into harmony with the Briand-Kellog Pact and to banish completely international warfare, is being considered by it."   It was he who, in 1927, appeared at the Preparatory Commission on Disarmament and startled the world by proposing the abolition of all military, air and naval forces, in which he got only the support of three nations which did not include Great Britain.

We heard Dolfuss, the "Pocket" Chancellor, make his brave speech which declared, in effect, that on no account would Austria be bludgeoned by Nazi Germany.   It was like watching David and Goliath, and he had a rousing reception when he began and when he ended.   Before the meeting of another Assembly he had been assassinated.

We missed by a few hours hearing Briand's eloquent speech advocating the Federation of Europe—he, the greatest orator of the League, but it fell on deaf ears.

We saw the millions of signatures on behalf of disarmament, collected throughout the world, in their glass cases built into the walls of the League's temporary building.

We watched the Press men crowding round Goebbels in 1933, and witnessed the boycott of the German delegation who carried round with them a nationalistic atmosphere, punctuated with Nazi salutes, which was quite alien to the spirit of Geneva.

Every year till he died, Count Apponyi asked the League what they had done to implement the Clemenceau letter by which the German representatives had been assured, before signing the Versailles Treaty, that the disarmament clauses were to be "the initiation of a general limitation of the armaments of all nations".

We saw a slim, dark figure walk up the middle aisle to record a vote in the ballot box on the rostrum and, as he went, all the spot-lights and all the cameras and all the pairs of eyes were turned on him for he was the chief delegate of Abyssinia. When he resumed his seat Sir Samuel Hoare went across and shook him by the hand with marked cordiality.

We heard Italy's Foreign Secretary, Aloisi, with obvious embarrassment and distaste, presenting his country's case with regard to Abyssinia. We were sitting in a hotel lounge the same evening when he came into it and stood about waiting for someone. He looked haggard and dispirited, for it is not easy to stand at the bar of the world's judgment with a bad case. Leyton went up to him and said, " Some of us felt sorry for you this morning in having such a case to put before the Assembly." He replied with a weary, wintry smile, " We can only hope some good may come out of it all in the end."

What came out of it in the end was expressed by Mr. te Water of South Africa in words which he addressed to the League a few months later :

> Fifty nations, led by three of the most powerful nations in the world, are about to declare their powerlessness to protect the weakest in their midst from destruction. The authority of the League is about to come to nought.

What came out of it was a death blow, dealt to the League, by the League. What that means in world history was presented to the League Assembly by that living embodiment of " J'Accuse ", Haile Selassie, in his moving and memorable speech, which included :

> I, Haile Selassie I, Emperor of Ethiopia, am here to-day to claim that justice that is due to my people, and the assistance promised to it eight months ago by fifty-two nations who asserted that an act of aggression had been committed in violation of international treaties. None other than the Emperor can address the appeal of the Ethiopian people to those fifty-two nations. . . . Statements have just been made in their respective Parliaments by the Governments of certain powers, the most influential Members of the League of Nations, that, since the aggressor has succeeded in occupying a large part of Ethiopian territory, they propose not to continue the application of any of the economic and financial measures decided upon against

the Italian Government. . . . I assert that the issue before the Assembly to-day is a much wider one. It is not merely a question of a settlement in the matter of Italian aggression. It is a question of collective security; of the very existence of the League; of the trust placed by States in international treaties; of the value of promises made to small States that their integrity and their independence shall be respected and assured. . . . It is international morality which is at stake. . . . Apart from the Kingdom of God, there is not on this earth any nation that is higher than any other. . . . God and history will remember your judgment.

God and history surely have remembered.

The night before the Assembly there is a service in the Cathedral at Geneva. In 1935 Dr. Hutton, editor of the *British Weekly*, was the preacher. He stated that the conception behind a League of Nations is an essential political expression of Christianity, but that Christ was crucified because he declared that God loved the *world*, rather than any chosen nations in it.

On our way to Geneva in the year 1935 we had a holiday in Corsica. There many French veterans sat in the sun outside their white-washed cottages smoking their long pipes, and playing cards. We found that the eyes of these old men were turned towards England. "What is England going to do?" they asked. "Is there to be war again?" "That depends on England." "What will England say at Geneva?"

Just before we left Corsica we had a week-end in Calvi. There as we sat on the water-front in the dusk we saw the Prince of Wales come ashore with a nice looking woman. Not only was she nice to look upon but she looked nice. Next day we learnt that she was Mrs. Simpson, whose existence we had never heard of till that moment. They joined a little crowd outside an open-air café where, in the light of oil flares, a French poilu as part of an impromptu concert, was giving a very funny impersonation of Hitler addressing his Black Guard.

In 1932 Leyton had crossed the Atlantic on a German liner where he was the only Britisher travelling in the 2nd Class, the rest being mostly German and American businessmen. As usual, he spent much of the voyage in the smoke room gathering any impressions he could from conversations. He notes in his diary that talk was mainly about the economic depression and that the general opinion seemed to be that Great Britain was better off and steadier than any other country. He writes that:

> The Americans are apprehensive but confident. The Germans on the other hand neither hope nor despair: they are just patient: things are as bad as can be and whether, therefore, the future is for Hitler or Britain, why worry? It is no use their veering one way or the other so long as they are in the grip of the Peace Treaties, and the initiative therefore lies with others: all they need to do is to sit back and wait until others crash as they have done. That seems to be the general attitude of German businessmen on board.

We had been to Germany twice between the wars, and in 1935 we decided to get " a sniff of the wind " in Berlin as far as it was possible for two Britishers who only had a smattering of German between them, which was of course a grave limitation, but we had many introductions to key people and depended on the educated German's almost invariable ability to speak English. We did have most illuminating contacts with both Nazis and those bitterly opposed to the Nazi régime. Everywhere we asked questions and listened, with little comment, to the answers. We had tea with Dr. von Schnee the ex-Governor of German East Africa and ex-Colonial Secretary under the Kaiser. He had already expressed himself in favour of universal mandates for all colonies. He was sore at the British judgment of Germany's unfitness for colonial rule and asked Leyton why it was: the latter suggested that the new Nazi theories of race were hardly a qualification. We had tea with the Committee of the Academic section of the ex-Servicemen's Association, five middle-aged men who all spoke English. Here, too, we found that a feeling of isolation was predominant. They could not understand why German ex-servicemen were not admitted to the international ex-servicemen's organization: they said the British were willing but the French vote had vetoed it: could anything more be done from the British end? Leyton undertook at least to report their point of view to the headquarters of the British Legion. One of these men was an architect with a special interest in town planning and had visited Birmingham to see the new housing estates. Another was in the history department of Berlin University and had made a special study of peace treaties and said, sadly, that most peace treaties contained in them the seeds of the next war, but he made one exception—the Peace Treaty between

Great Britain and South Africa at the close of the Boer War. We got the impression that these men were far from being Nazis.

We did, on the other hand, meet some very strong Nazis to whom Hitler was a god. A young doctor in the Health Department, with whom we had an appointment, insisted on walking with us to our next, rhapsodizing all the way : "Hitler is the greatest German who ever lived. All I can do and be for him could never be enough." When asked if Hitler had room in his régime for the old, the sick, the infirm and the mentally deranged, his reply was, " The Fuehrer loves every German, but only the young have strength enough to give to making the new and better Germany that is to be." We were told how Hitler had " taken the cloak from his own shoulders and put it round a poor, ill-clad old man in a crowd ; and how little children always loved him ".

We had an interview with the second in command in the new Women's Movement, a tall, fair-haired young woman who, we had been told elsewhere, had failed in her finals as a barrister before the Hitler régime closed the legal profession to her sex. We asked why there were no longer women in the Reichstag. She replied that the Fuehrer had such a reverence for womanhood that he thought "the dirty work of Parliamentary life unsuitable " : that he wanted to protect women, and was grieved by the ribaldry which had crept into German life so that even a pregnant woman could be a matter of jocularity, and that already he had purified and uplifted the attitude of the people on such matters.

Another woman, just back from a speaking tour in Britain, wife of a General, when we asked her the same question about women and the Reichstag replied, " But what should they do there? Men can do it just as well." When pressed further, " The women put Clara Zetkin into the Reichstag in the old days : we want no more of her sort," on which Leyton commented to me afterwards, " which is like saying that if one electric light bulb is defective it is best to scrap the whole system and go back to candles ".

We met a number of women of another kind, women bitterly opposed to Hitler and scornful of his attitude to their sex. Some of these, as members of committees of women's societies, had dissolved their organizations overnight rather than submit to having their Minutes scrutinized and a Nazi representative sent to attend every meeting of their committees. Among these societies were

the National Council of Women, and the Women's International
League. These women ran grave risks in the attitude they took :
we marvelled at the trust they showed in us by disclosing their
feelings so freely. These, and men like them, reiterated over and
over again, "Don't let Britain concede anything to Hitler : it will
be a disaster if you do." They were in the depths of depression,
almost of despair, at the state of their Fatherland, and felt isolated
from the outside world. They felt hopeless because when more
liberal elements had been in power after the 1914-18 war there had
been little or no encouragement, no response and no helping hands
held out politically from other countries. Charitable relief came and
they were deeply grateful for it, but that was not enough.

We met both Jews and anti-Semites. The former were smarting
under the most terrible injustices even then ; the latter making the
same two accusations against the Jews over and over again : first,
that the Jews of Central Europe had crowded in after 1918 and hit
them while they were down by buying up real estate and business
concerns when the mark was depreciated ; second, that if a Jew
were put into any position of authority he always filled the vacancies
under him with other Jews, and that Gentiles were crowded out.
They ruefully acknowledged the intellectual ability and industry of
the Jews, and one strong anti-Semite said that, much as he had hated
to do it, he had been obliged to engage a Jewish lawyer to fight his
case against another Jew as otherwise he would certainly have lost it !

In the midst of the turmoils, the friction, the suspicions, and the
mutual recriminations of Berlin was a little oasis of peace and trust
and understanding in the Quaker Centre, with Corder and Gwen
Catchpool in charge of it. A non-Friend once remarked in another
context (it was about Woodbrooke), what a rest it was to come out
of the ordinary world into a community where Yea meant Yea
and Nay meant Nay and where you could trust your fellow man.
So it was in the Friends Centre in Berlin in 1935. Not that the
surrounding suspicion and spying left this little community
untouched. The private house of Corder and Gwen Catchpool,
out in the suburbs, was raided by Nazi agents, and each of them was
kept for hours at the two ends of their living room under guard,
while the whole house was searched from attic to cellar. Corder had
no fear for himself but was in an agony of apprehension lest any of
the Jewish and other anti-Nazis who had trusted him might be

incriminated by papers found in his possession. After the search he was marched away, leaving Gwen in great anxiety as to what was happening to him. He was brought safely home again after a short period. They discovered that they had been denounced to the authorities by their own German domestic worker, who had reported that there were "queer goings-on in that house, and many queer people coming to it". It seemed to me a signal example of the Quaker way of life that the Catchpools continued to employ her, speaking of her to others quietly and peaceably as one who had been misled, and was too ignorant and foolish to realize what she had done. She continued to share their family meals but she eventually ceased to come ; she evidently felt ill at ease, for human beings seldom like or are happy with those they have injured. Corder and Gwen Catchpool did marvellously understand, and put themselves into the position of, others whose sense of duty was utterly at variance with their own. From what we saw and heard during our visit, they were making an outstanding contribution to the Berlin of those troublous times by their own spirit and way of life.

We moved on from Berlin first to Fulda, and then to a mountain-top in the Principality of Lichtenstein, to see for ourselves the interesting experiment in Christian living known as the Bruderhof. We had first got to know about it when the son of the founder, Eberhard Arnold, while studying at Birmingham University, had frequented Carrs Lane and had had considerable influence among some young people, of whom several eventually joined. After the tension of Berlin, where we were afraid to speak freely in a restaurant, and afraid lest we might inadvertently give away information gleaned from one person to the next, it was like leaving a prison and going out into pure, fresh air to arrive at the Rhôn Bruderhof. In spite of the fact that the Brothers were in danger all the time, and suffering real privation there was a serenity and even a gaiety about the community which was at once apparent. I had never personally been in close contact with people who had taken such risks and undergone such physical sacrifices for what they believed. Many people are willing to suffer themselves, far fewer are willing that their children should suffer. A short time before we got to Fulda the Community had heard that they were no longer to be allowed to teach their own children but that a qualified Nazi teacher would be arriving to take charge of the school in a few days' time. It was decided by the

Community that under no circumstances must their children's minds be diverted from the pure truth of Christianity and poisoned by Nazi doctrine. So the day before the teacher was due to arrive two adults and the twenty children of school age crossed the frontier into Switzerland, where there had been no time to make provision and, indeed, there were practically no material resources to make provision with : they had only one or two addresses of sympathizers as security against homelessness and want. But the security proved sufficient. When, at Fulda, the Nazi teacher arrived he was greeted with cordiality, shown round the estate, shown the school building : then, when having completed his tour, he said, " And where are the children? " they replied, " Our children have gone to Switzerland for a long visit." He was out of work before he had begun.

At the time we got to Fulda the Community was facing another problem and was anxious to talk it over with Leyton. Word had reached them that conscription was imminent which would affect thirty of their young men. The question to be decided was : Would it be running away from their witness and their duty if they, too, went over the frontier to the branch of the Bruderhof already in its initial stages in Lichtenstein? Everything was referred back to the Gospels and it seemed to them there was good authority for " fleeing to the mountains ". Momma Eberhard, wife of the leader, with her kerchiefed head and wearing her peasant dress, had a simple grandeur about her as she said gravely, " Do not think we act in a panic. If we think it right for our young people to stay, they stay ; if to go, then they will go with everything quietly made ready." She added that a strong reason against their staying was that no testimony would be made possible thereby : they would just disappear, never to return, and only their friends would guess what had happened to them. It was finally decided that it would be right for them to go, for none of them was willing to be conscripted or to bear arms in any circumstances.

In Lichtenstein, in a disused hotel surrounded by deep snow, on top of a 6,000 feet mountain, we visited the children who had been taken out of Germany, and the adults looking after them. They were living on the lowest possible diet but again there was the same impression of being in a joyful, carefree community, reminding us of Thomas à Kempis, " He who has but one aim, and refers all things to one Principle, and views all things in one light, is able to abide steadfast, and to rest in God." Leyton's diary has comments and impressions :

> An all-pervading sense of quiet joy and peace, and—despite a precarious and meagre provision of necessities—a complete faith which banishes even a trace of anxiety. It is all the time what a Church meeting (in the Congregational sense) is at its best ; but it covers all life's affairs as no Church meeting does. Nevertheless the Community (though in principle repudiating the un-Christian ways of the world, and in practice succeeding as far as its internal economy is concerned) depends for support and for many of its services upon the outside world—financial gifts or gifts in kind : telephone, transport, purchases, sales, etc. From a business point of view, the Community life appears slack ; and no balance sheet was produced. [Though they constantly ask for money. E.R.R.] . . . The fuller Christian life of the members is partly due to the removal of the Community from the complexities of the world's life. Points of compromise are thereby reduced in number. . . . The Community is a terrific challenge in its single-minded search for the Will of God in Christ at any cost. . . . But the question we kept putting was : " Is it *the* way or *a* way? " Of the latter we felt quite sure but not at all prepared to believe the former.

We could never get a direct answer. It was this lack of tolerance which seemed to us the great gap in the Christian witness of the Bruderhof and subsequent experience has confirmed this initial impression.

With regard to their continual money-raising efforts, one of them told us that begging was nothing to be ashamed of when you yourself had given your all and had nothing more you could give.

Chapter XV

WOODBROOKE AND QUAKERISM

THE DEVELOPMENT IN Leyton which finally led him, in 1946, to join the Society of Friends was a gradual one, extending over a number of years. His biography has been punctuated, from Melbourne days onwards, with references to his contacts with Quakerism and his sense of unity with its outlook. As early as 1934, during his Sabbatical year, on the few Sundays when he was in Birmingham, we attended one or other of the Friends' Meetings. After one of these, I heard him say to a member outside the Meeting House : " I feel very much inclined to apply for membership of the Society ; I am so much at home among you." She gently, but incisively, steered him back whence he came by saying, " You stay where you are : you are more needed there than here."

It was still twelve years before he took the final step, and the process leading to it was not a simple one.

Carrs Lane was generous in its recognition of his concern to serve the cause of peace, involving frequent periods of absence, though I doubt whether most members had more than a vague idea of exactly what he was doing when away. On several occasions he was one of a team of lecturers at American Summer Schools on International Relations, organized by American Friends but not chiefly for Friends. The lecturers included politicians, newspaper men, college professors, psychologists, a novelist and, for more than one session, Mrs. F. D. Roosevelt. Leyton supplied the political-religious element and not only did he deliver series of lectures but he added hours of discussion. Every evening, till darkness fell, he would be found on the College campus surrounded by a group of students of all ages peppering him with questions on international and religious problems. I remember a middle-aged Jewish newspaper editor saying at the end of one such discussion period : " If Christianity is like this then I want to be a Christian." Leyton found great zest in these summer schools and believed that they were fruitful. On the voyage home on two occasions I remember how the shadow of sermon preparation seemed to fall upon him as we got nearer to the shores of England. He still believed in the Church's obligation to preach and in the efficacy of preaching ; but, after these lecture tours and their obvious fruitfulness, he came to feel that he himself was trying to put into sermon form material which could much more easily be expressed in another form. He thought that the excessive labour he found in sermon preparation was due to forcing into that medium material which needed another. As a concomitant of this, the farther we got from the heat and the sunshine of the U.S.A. and the nearer to the damp and the clouds of Britain another shadow fell upon him : Would he be able to get through two services on his first Sunday, or would his throat let him down? Reaching the home port was not unsullied joy, but, after one Sunday's services safely carried through, the clouds thinned if they did not entirely disperse. This tendency to doubt sermon-making as the most fruitful use of his own time and energy was, I believe, one of the strands leading to Quakerism.

Another was his attitude towards the sacraments. In a pamphlet he published on Church Membership for intending members, he wrote :

> Neither baptism nor the communion service nor any other form of worship can be a test of churchmanship, for these are merely symbolic aids to our spiritual nurture and are valued as such by most Christians (though they are not helpful to all); and consequently the failure to utilize them cannot bar out from the Church a person whose character and life give evidence of vital Christian faith.

Dr. Dale before him had taken the same attitude. It was one which prepared him for the Friends' emphasis on inward realities —"We who set aside the outward ought to make sure that we do know the inward realities."*

His affinity to Quakerism was recognized by Friends in 1939 when he was offered a year's Fellowship at Woodbrooke, the Quaker International College on the outskirts of Birmingham, in order to give him leisure and opportunity to write. This invitation came just as he was cut off by throat trouble from any ministry involving constant use of his voice in public buildings. For this, and many other reasons, he gladly accepted, and we moved to a small house close to Woodbrooke. The written work finally emerged as the

* Elizabeth Braithwaite Emmott: *The Story of Quakerism.*

Swarthmore Lecture on "Planning for Freedom", delivered at Yearly Meeting in 1943. But the writing of it was delayed by the outbreak of war and by the call of Carrs Lane to return for part-time work, which, he believed, a new method of voice production then made possible.

A year later, just before the beginning of the Autumn Term in 1940, he was asked to undertake still further responsibilities in Woodbrooke. The Warden, Henry T. Cadbury, was in poor health and his doctor advised at least a term off duty and we were asked to go into residence and carry on the Wardenship and Leyton also to lecture. This temporary arrangement was prolonged, term by term, till we ended by having resident charge of Woodbrooke for four years, during all of which war conditions prevailed. It was the first time in his life that Leyton had lived in a residential community, except for a few weeks at a time. It was a deeply interesting and, at the same time, an exhausting experience. The usual students who came to Woodbrooke from overseas were no longer available in any numbers ; in the good old days, in one term, there might be as many as twenty-two nationalities represented among those in residence ; we never mustered more than eleven. Distinguished visitors, including Mr. Gandhi and Rabindranath Tagore, had stayed at Woodbrooke : now among our visitors were twenty-three bombed-out people from the back streets of Birmingham. Our students included medicals evacuated from King's College, London, and many refugees from Nazi oppression, and some conscientious objectors. Young people came to study at the University who had no knowledge of, or interest in, Quakerism. When asked if she knew any Quakers, one new student, after thinking for some time, said she thought it must have been a Quaker who showed them round Swarthmore Hall where she had been on a school visit. I believe most who came and used Woodbrooke as a hostel during those war years, left with some interest at least in the Quaker way of life. But I believe Woodbrooke's greatest wartime service was to provide a haven for refugees from Europe, where they could look for understanding, where they could have time to recover in part from bitter experiences, and make the exacting adjustments required of them ; a place, too, where members of nations at enmity could meet each other, and even, after a time, put their own case forward and hope for, at least, patient hearing.

It was no small achievement to have living under one roof in time of war, Czechs and Sudetan Germans, Poles and Germans and French and, for the most part, living in harmony.

During the autumn of 1940, raids were heavy and continuous in Birmingham, and the responsibility for the Woodbrooke community, spread over its rambling, complicated buildings, was a heavy one. We spent many nights in the cellar, which had been reinforced as a shelter. Every time there was a warning Leyton went on duty and lack of sleep was one of his greatest trials. A colleague on the staff wrote about him in the *Woodbrooke Journal*:

> The heavy blitz experiences brought many practical emergencies —endless arranging of fire watchers, dealing with police, indoor and outdoor floods and other fabric troubles. For a convinced pacifist who felt all war to be wrong, it was a trial of patience to have to spend long nights in the cellar crowded with students, or to patrol in a tin helmet and keep a constant supervision of black-out, but the cheery way in which he carried through all these necessities and the daily round of work as well was an example to us all. . . . It was said he was a " Bonnie Fighter for Peace "—yet perhaps in the end it was not so much his argument as his living embodiment of friendship with all that made the lasting impression even on those who disagreed with him.

Underneath his invariably cheerful exterior he had his moods of depression which he revealed only to a few. He unburdened himself in a letter to his brother in the U.S.A. in 1940 :

> We have had one of the finest and most beautiful summers I ever remember in England and normally I should have revelled in the open-air life and the opportunity of enjoying the long balmy twilight. But somehow it seems a crime to enjoy anything too much. And furthermore one's nerves are all the time on the alert. The finer the day the more is the chance of air-raids and one's ears are unconsciously cocked all the time for gun-fire. I know it is silly and we fight against it, but it is the constant background of all we do. . . . The lack of sleep is a terribly wearing thing and it sets temper on edge. . . . The imbecility of the whole thing would be unbelievable were it not so tragically real, for we are doing just the same to unoffending German citizens with our aircraft. . . . What fools these mortals be ! Yet now we are in it what else can be done? The alternatives have crystallized out starkly and clearly : either you must take the pacifist way or the military way, and if you don't take

the one you must—and ought to—take the other for anything else would be craven and cowardly. . . . No one stops to think what victory means or whether if we win the war we shall lose the peace, as we did in 1918. "No one?" Yes, a few despised pacifists, but they are voices crying in the wilderness. . . . It all seems so impersonal somehow. . . . Yet I never knew a public temper so determined about anything. "No truck with the Dictators" is the motto and there will be none whatever the cost. Meantime, the achievements of the R.A.F. boys (they are little more) fill one with amazement and admiration. . . . The boys are the victims of an international system which could have been transformed years ago if we had had statesmen worthy of the name. Well, it's no use grousing. We just carry on as best we can, and try to preserve the temper which will be prepared for a decent peace when the time comes.

That is the letter of Leyton Richards as he was when weighed down by a sense of the tragic failure of statesmen, and especially of Christians, to find an alternative to war, over-strained by constant air raids, tired out by want of sleep.

The Woodbrooke years gave him still closer touch with Quakerism and he saw more and more to attract him. He had worked with them, thought like them, found support from them in causes which were to him of first importance. It is not surprising, therefore, that in the end he found his way to them. In applying for membership in 1946 he wrote :

For over thirty years I have had intimate contact with Friends in common work of various kinds, and feel that I both understand and share their outlook in essential things. Membership of the Society, accordingly, would be for me the natural outcome of these contacts.

His application was accepted and at the same time he made it clear to the two Friends who were his official visitors that he did not repudiate his past. He wrote simultaneously to Dr. Sidney Berry, as Secretary of the Congregational Union of England and Wales, asking of he might still remain on the list of Congregational ministers. The Committee of the Union, responsible for such decisions, was unanimous in consenting to this. He had been a loyal Congregationalist but never a keen denominationalist though he believed that Congregationalism has had and still has a great contribution to make to the Church as a whole, and to the training of citizens in responsible self-government. He valued particularly, and had reverence for, the Congregational conception of the Church Meeting, which he regarded as the focal point of a Congregational Church's life. He agreed, with Friends, that no vote should be taken on any matter involving principle : that guidance by a majority was not necessarily guidance of the Spirit. He introduced this conception into the Carrs Lane Church Meeting but never felt that it was universally acceptable or appreciated there. As regards the linking of the independent, entirely self-governing, local Churches into the larger body of the Congregational Union, he recognized that this was necessary and an expedient which should be loyally accepted. But he had least sympathy with Congregationalism *en masse*, and especially when it expressed itself in large-scale "rallies" and "demonstrations". He believed in a minimum of organization and a maximum of patient solid work within the local congregations and was convinced that all would be well with the Union if there was spiritual health in the units which composed it. He worried and grieved about the pitiful underpayment of many of his brother ministers. He was himself a conscientious giver and had perhaps too great faith in finding the same standard in his fellow members. So he hated begging or launching appeals. It was his way rather to announce a collection tersely, as he did, for Rhondda Valley Relief, in Bowdon Downs, with four words : " Sirs, ye are brethren," and on that occasion it proved adequate. Treasurers, hoping to induce him to be eloquent in support of some special appeal, entered the Vestry treading like Agag, and often came out disappointed. He would not accept the fact that his own conscience in these matters was unusually sensitive. A short time after he died his banker, who knew all his financial affairs intimately, departed from his accustomed formality of manner and burst out, " My word, he *was* a Christian : we have never had a client like him and I don't suppose we ever shall." He had the most exacting views on what was legitimate in investment, rate of interest, personal expenditure and so on. Along with this high standard for himself went acute embarrassment in asking others for money, so that he was only half-hearted in the launching of denominational and other funds. He believed that large hearts and deep religious convictions and tender consciences were a much more reliable source of income for good objects than eloquent appeals, long purses and elaborate organization. And he always preferred giving to be anonymous, as it often is in Congregational churches.

He was never entirely happy in the May Meetings of the Congregational Union : he used to feel sometimes that they were fiddling while Rome was burning : and he particularly disliked the inclusion on their programmes of men who were leading politicians rather than Christian leaders.   A number of men in different parts of the country in 1938 expressed their wish to nominate him for the chair of the Union but he refused to let his name go forward because, as he wrote, if elected :

> I should have to forego practically every other public activity for the time being. . . .   The issues of war and peace are in the balance . . .   On account of a long and varied experience in regard to international affairs, I feel I am better fitted to serve the Church Universal in that connection than by devoting myself exclusively to the interests of one denomination.

He was a loyal Congregationalist and took his share in the local work of the denomination but he was never zealous for Congregationalism and, I believe, he would not have become zealous for Quakerism though he would have been a loyal Quaker.   Once he attended Friends Meetings regularly he came to appreciate greatly both the silence, and the building up of several contributions into a unified whole, which had a value and completeness of religious experience and expression other than could have been achieved through a single mind.   He appreciated, too, the pauses between the various contributions which gave time to absorb one idea before passing to another.   At the same time he missed the fruits of systematic, disciplined thinking and of solid, scholarly Bible study which should be the background to any meeting for worship.   He felt more than ever how much the different branches of the Christian Church have to give to each other and to learn from one another. In becoming a Friend he found personal happiness and rest : no longer did he need to strive for values which, he felt, were in danger of being overlooked.   The warrior had come home and was at peace, but he never regretted his years of warfare.

After his death a joint Minute was passed by Birmingham and Reading Friends which includes some sentences I should like to quote :

> He was accepted for Membership by Warwickshire Monthly Meeting in 1946.   He attended Selly Oak Meeting where his presence was deeply valued.   It was noticeable how truly this gifted preacher

understood the spirit of the Quaker way of worship and the value of the silence. . . . His vocal contributions, brief and to the point, arose from the exercise of the meeting and led into a deeper experience of truth. When he . . . left Birmingham his Warwickshire friends felt the loss of one whose deep, joyous faith had made it easier for others to believe in God. . . . His ministry in Reading was fresh and illuminating, and was especially appreciated by the boys of Leighton Park School. Though his residence among Reading Friends was short, its influence cannot be measured by time ; it will always be remembered with deep thankfulness by those who were privileged to meet him.

Chapter XVI

LAST PHASE

For the sword outgrows its sheath
And the soul wears out the breast
And the heart must pause to breathe
And love itself have rest.

Byron.

JUST AFTER EASTER in 1945, on his way home from a week-end of preaching and speaking at his old Church, Bowdon Downs, Leyton had a heart attack, and was confined to his room for several weeks. When visitors, strictly limited in number, came to see him he was so cheerful and lively that he gave little impression of being ill. After a time he picked up and went about again in our own neighbourhood and, once a week, went into Birmingham where he usually attended a lunch for supporters of Federal Union. He found it a great tax to go into the city, whereas he seemed to draw strength from the country and once he had got there, often with difficulty, he could outwalk me. After a time, therefore, it seemed wise to look for a house in the country, away from the noise and rush, the wear and tear of city life, and away from the telephone calls continually asking him to undertake speaking and preaching engagements for which he no longer had the strength. We wanted, too, to be within easier reach of our three daughters and our son-in-law and two small grandsons, all of whom lived in London or the Home Counties.

Our eyes turned towards Berkshire because he knew and loved that county, because we already had a small circle of friends and acquaintances in Reading and because there was a good Friends Meeting there, and also because our family would be within easy reach. After prolonged search we were fortunate in securing a pleasant bungalow and garden, at Mortimer Common, seven miles out of Reading, close to the Hampshire boundary, and with a good bus service. We moved in September 1947 and the change of environment meant a revolution in our way of life, and seemed to bring renewed health and strength to Leyton. With characteristic thoroughness he began straight away to learn to be retired and a countryman. He joined the Village Produce Association; he attended meetings of the Parish Council ; he bought and studied books on fruit and vegetable growing, on pests and fertilizers and compost heaps ; he drew neat and elaborate plans for the lay-out and rotation of crops in our vegetable plot. Before we came to Mortimer he had announced his intention of doing no gardening and the assurance that help would be available had been one of the conditions of our moving to the new house. But within a few weeks, with the heavier work being done for him, he was working in the garden for part of most days. And every day we went for a country walk, and, by study of maps, he found lovely paths and pools which older inhabitants had missed. He took a share of the housework, too, doing it with the thoroughness and meticulous care with which he attacked every kind of task which came his way. No highly-trained parlourmaid ever expended more purposeful energy in scraping and stacking, rinsing and polishing dishes than he did whenever he washed up.

I had been afraid he would badly miss the manifold and stimulating contacts of Birmingham, which he had only left behind with reluctance, but I need not have worried. For one thing a surprising number of our friends and relations found it possible to visit us, so that we never felt cut off. And we were seeing more of our family in a more leisured way than had been possible for many years ; hardly a week-end passed without one or other of them coming home. The claim of his children on an over-busy public man's time often has to come last. Now it was going to be possible to redress the balance in the happiest circumstances.

We had left behind the city pavements with their hurrying crowds, the sprawling suburban streets, and the never ceasing undertones of heavy traffic. Our new house faced a common covered with gorse and broom ; close by were woods, and open stretches of bracken and heather ; the stillness of the nights was only broken by the sound of winds and trees and birds. Once, when I foolishly asked him if he felt bored, he replied with well deserved scorn, " Bored, *bored* ? Of course not. I can't get over our good fortune in being here and ending our days like this." We were beginning to make new contacts of a different kind. In the lanes the older country folk looked at us with caution and gave us a passing greeting. More than one of them watched our amateur gardening over the fence in reserved silence but, when invited, made such remarks as, " Those onions are set wrong," or, " It's too late to save your broad beans now," or, more helpfully, " I'll bring something round that'll make those peas grow like a miracle," or, " A gardener must learn patience. The sun will shine again some day."

On most Sunday mornings we went into Reading to attend Friends Meeting and were soon made to feel part of it. The boys of Leighton Park School, a Friends' boarding school, attend it and I have had testimonies to the value to them, and to others, of Leyton's vocal ministry, sparingly exercised in Meeting from time to time. In July 1948, when he had been a member there for only nine months, he was asked to become an Elder, and he accepted with appreciation.

So our days passed pleasantly, with friends and relations coming and going, till we had been in our new home for eleven months and had made many improvements in it to fit our tastes and our needs. The garden, in spite of its very stony soil, flourished under Leyton's scientific care and he became increasingly interested in it as he began to see the fruits of his own labour, and of his vigilant fight against the procession of garden enemies which attacked it. The scarlet runners he had himself sown were rioting round their tall stakes, the apples and damsons he had protected from pests were showing a good harvest, and the winter vegetables were well established. All this open-air occupation left no detachment for work at his desk but he intended to devote the coming winter months to writing.

For three years part of his mind had calmly accepted the fact that his hold on life was precarious, but though he had been, over the years, inclined to be pre-occupied with minor ailments, he showed little pre-occupation with the much more serious condition which had now developed. His zeal in the garden often outran his physical strength and in the third week in August he showed unmistakable signs of over-fatigue, and I persuaded him, much against his inclination, to take a few days' rest in bed. There he stayed during Friday and Saturday, reading Gunther's *Inside U.S.A.*, and showing a lively concern in the doings of the household. The day he went to bed, Joyce and one of our grandsons arrived for a week's visit, bringing with them another small boy. The latter proved a keen young naturalist and on Saturday afternoon Leyton helped him to identify flowers and insects for a collection he was making, and both were quite absorbed in this common interest. Later, when the boys had gone to bed, he and Joyce and I talked happily of many things till he was ready to settle for the night, comfortable and serene.

Just after midnight he had a severe heart attack which caused prostrating weakness and discomfort but, mercifully, no severe pain. Ill as he was, he expressed his regret to the doctor at the necessity for calling him out during the night. About 2 a.m., while I was alone with him, he died. He had lived fully, eagerly, richly, to the very end.

In a book of devotions he was using at that time was a card marking the place ; on it, copied by his own hand, were some words from Livingstone's *Last Journal* : " I leave my cause and all my concerns in the hands of God. I feel quite calm in that confidence."

On Sunday afternoon we got in touch with Birmingham friends, for I wanted Leyton's Memorial Service to be at Carrs Lane, the Church to which he had given the longest years of his ministry. I knew he wished to have private cremation with as little concentration as possible on the body he would by then have discarded. Loyal Friend though he had become, he had certain reservations about the Quaker way of conducting both weddings and funerals. He felt that they sometimes lacked sufficient, explicit, spoken, reference to those solid Christian foundations in the strength of which, he believed, life and death, joy and grief can best be met ; and they missed the wordless comfort and the ageless beauty of great music. And yet I knew that, as he had died in true fellowship with both Quakers and Congregationalists, both must somehow have their place in any memorial service. Reading and Birmingham Friends showed wonderfully delicate appreciation of the difficulty of combining the two ways of worship and members of Carrs Lane were just as much concerned.

At the Reading Crematorium three members of Reading Friends' Monthly Meeting joined the intimate family circle. It seemed appropriate also that two old friends should be present from the Church of his boyhood, Trinity Congregational Church, Mr. and Miss Grigsby, and two old friends, Mr. and Miss Goulty, represented old associations with Bowdon Downs. The Rev. Gordon Smailes of Trinity conducted a simple, dignified service and gave an address on " The Happy Warrior ". On the coffin were gay, old-fashioned cottage garden flowers, with a spray of heather.

On Wednesday members of the family circle were united with a large company of people at Carrs Lane at the service which had been announced in the Press as a Meeting for Worship. H. G. Wood, representing Friends, and Alan G. Knott, representing Congregationalists, both spoke and the present minister of Carrs Lane, the Rev. Leslie Tizard, took part. Beside them on the rostrum were Edward Cadbury and Wilfrid Littleboy from Selly Oak Friends' Meeting, and the deacons of Carrs Lane. The music was beautiful and comforting, especially the singing of Bach's " Jesu, Joy of Man's Desiring ", the words of which seemed to crystallize the centre of Leyton's life here on earth.

One friend wrote to me just after his death : " There will be mourning for him all over the world," and he was right. Letters, telegrams, cablegrams poured in upon us and it was brought home to us more than ever that the world had been his parish. We were struck with the recurrence of legal and of military metaphors in the letters of sympathy. Friends wrote of him as an " Advocate of Christ " ; as " one who sifted true from false evidence and built for men an impregnable Christian case ". Several spoke of him as " the Happy Warrior ", or as " One who never turned his back, but marched breast forward ", as " One who blew the Lord's trumpet, but never his own ". Many times he was depicted as having the Sword of the Spirit in his hand. His rallying cry during his life had always been, " Soldiers of the Cross arise ", and it was as a " good soldier of Jesus Christ " that his fellow men honoured him in death.

*　　　*　　　*　　　*

And now this story of a life is finished.   Death came swiftly and gathered up youth and age, beginnings and endings, days and years, and bound them in one.   In the completeness Death has brought, it is possible to turn back and see how each page led on to the next and and each made a contribution to the whole.

When the mists of time clear and intimations of immortality come shining through, then I believe that all that was Leyton Richards here on earth still goes on, raised and fulfilled, that he has outlived time and space in which he served for a season and that he keeps his distinguishing marks about him still—his scars and his blemishes as well as his virtues and his graces, the eagerness of his youth, the turbulence of his middle years, his mellow autumn bringing with it "the wisdom of a fiery heart which has learned patience", his gentleness and his sternness, his deep affections and his abiding loyalties, his sorrow at the sin of the world and his "cheerfulness that was always breaking in", his triumphant faith in God and in man which was born of his own faithfulness.

And we who are left need not lose him for "you can lose a man like that by your own death but not by his".

Appendix

Quotations from the many letters and tributes received after his death :

FROM SOME WHO LISTENED TO HIM AS YOUNG PEOPLE

" In our home we always called him—' Never will, never shall '—a favourite phrase of his when he was preaching. My recollection of Sunday evenings is wanting to get out of church to get going ahead with what he was urging me to do."

" At an impressionable period of my life when I might easily have been deflected from Christianity by the mawkish way it is so often presented, I was privileged to hear his vigorous and challenging interpretation of the Gospel."

" To him I owe—more than to any other man—what training in honest and critical thinking I was able to absorb and a great longing to emulate his capacity for patience with those searching for conviction."

FROM A MISSIONARY

" In those days the impact of Christianity on my own life was fresh and I brought a critical mind to sermons and a still more critical eye to the preacher. His were by any test good sermons : direct and thoughtful, with a clear implication that the concern of the Christian stretched world-wide and the standard of all judgment was the mind of Christ. He took loyalty to the Christian position seriously and assumed that any sincere Christian would do likewise."

FROM A MIDDLE-AGED WIFE AND MOTHER

" So much gets over-laid and rusty and dim with these years of hard living, but the things which were made so clear and right when we were young by Leyton Richards will always be a guide to our thinking and living."

FROM A MIDDLE-AGED MAN

" After meetings in ———, at which clergy and ministers had been present, my father would say, ' Leyton Richards is head and shoulders above all of them.' I know now how true that judgment was. . . . In times of despair I have frequently thought, ' Well, at any rate, the world does contain Leyton Richards ' and I have felt strengthened and reassured to think of him."

FROM AN AUSTRALIAN MINISTER OF RELIGION

" Many people who were influenced by his pulpit work noted the fact that we left the service ' branded ' by one thought, and that thought stuck. As an instance of his capacity for doing in one sermon what other preachers would take many addresses to effect, I was, while a student, student-pastor of a small suburban Church. One of my Sunday School teachers, a clever, devout, young girl, was worried by certain views and superficial ideas then going about as to the teaching of the Old Testament. In my half-baked way I helped her and lent her such books as I had. Just then Mr. Richards was preaching a series of addresses to Sunday School teachers, one of which was on the subject, ' How shall I present the Old Testament in the light of to-day? ' She attended the service and heard the address and took it down in shorthand. Next Sunday she was back in her class. His perfect presentation of the subject had satisfied her and resolved her doubts."

FROM ANOTHER AUSTRALIAN

" To those of us who were young in those days, the coming to the Church of Mr. Richards was as the breath of spring. How we appreciated his vigorous and forceful preaching—the sermons so carefully prepared and always conveying a challenge. . . . His courageous crusade against the introduction in Australia of compulsory military training had an electrifying effect on the community, bringing much heart-searching and considerable distress of spirit. . . . Some did go all the way with him, but all, except those who were completely ' offended ' by the doctrine, were, through him, profoundly influenced in their thinking on the subject of war and peace."

FROM A MIDDLE-AGED WOMAN

" I can never forget how much his lead meant to some puzzled and rather lonely-feeling people in 1914-18."

FROM A MEMBER OF PARLIAMENT

" As a direct result of Leyton's inspiration and guidance I have found myself in Parliament with my life, as his was, devoted to that same great cause of peace. I have been given a purpose and a principle by a great Christian and, in his memory, I promise I will do all I can to fulfil it."

Appendix

"He never made us lesser, younger folk feel small. Indeed, he did the opposite and communicated something of his own vigour and strength —made us proud to do insignificant jobs eagerly and faithfully. There was such a wonderful dignity about his humility and no trace of stooping to befriend us. He was so utterly free, clean of snobbery that he enjoyed even people who couldn't hold a candle to him mentally or spiritually— all that was a part of his ruthless, brave rectitude, his clear direct judgment —delicate, accurate, fearless as a surgeon's knife. He knew with his soul, so that conviction was expressed in limpid, clear terms as refreshing as a mountain stream. . . . He had all the lovely simplicity of the modern—devoid of Victorian frills and airs, and all the strength and effectiveness that is the good tradition."

FROM ANOTHER CONGREGATIONAL MINISTER

"He and J. L. Paton were the two great men I have known, their public life and work the expression, and adequate expression, of their private personalities. The Colossus of Congregationalism has gone."

FROM A BUSINESS MAN

"I am a poor sort of religious man but I believe in the God whom Leyton preached and followed. What honest man could not be convinced by his compelling logic, and try to follow the downright Christian way of life which he preached and lived? "

FROM AN ECONOMIST

"He has given me more than any other living man has done—the power to believe. He fortified me not only for the day to come but for all days that came."

FROM A SCIENTIST

"His religion was the greatest interest and surprise to me as I have suffered much at the hands of orthodoxy and I rejoiced to find an intelligent and tolerant approach to a subject so full of prejudice. His own belief was a great encouragement to me."

FROM A PHILOSOPHER

"I should like to put on record . . . my own sense of obligation to him for having brought home to me more powerfully than any one has done before or since, the range and the relevance of the Christian faith."

Private View of a Public Man

The Times (August 31st, 1948). By the Bishop of Birmingham (Dr. E. W. Barnes):

" Of recent years, when he gave expression to the convictions which he had come to hold, he would speak with a prophetic authority which I have rarely heard equalled by any English religious teacher. In Birmingham his sincerity and courage, coupled with his intellectual ability and entire lack of self-seeking, made him a leader whose influence enlarged the great tradition of the Church which he served."

FROM A TRAM CONDUCTOR

" I feel that I should like to pay my small tribute to the memory of Mr. Richards. I write as somewhat of an outsider and also what is termed a working-man. I was a tram conductor in Birmingham in the time of Mr. Richards. I was one of those who sat in the back pews or a little diffidently half behind a pillar. Many times during these last years I have read the preaching appointments in the *Journal* and wondered when I should see Mr. Richards's name there again ; now, alas ! it will never appear again. Dr. Lynn Hough once said in prayer, referring to Carrs Lane, ' this place sanctified by generations of just men made perfect'. Another name is added to that great company, that cloud of witnesses, a good man made perfect.

" I never aspired to shake hands with Mr. Richards. I was content to worship from afar, yet that old saying about every man having his hero was never better illustrated than in me and Mr. Richards. In the pulpit he was very dignified yet restful, composed and always unhurried. After the singing of a hymn he always sat down with the congregation, sometimes he would sit quietly perhaps for a full minute or so, so that in that quiet pause one really did have that feeling of being away from the world.

" Of those wonderful sermons which he preached many are still retained in memory even to the text. Mr. Richards was what I should describe as a New Testament man, he rarely read or took a text from the Old Testament.

" I should like to close my faltering tribute with some simple words from Hardy's novel, *The Woodlanders*. On the last page, Marty South, at the grave of Giles Winterbourne, says, ' For you was a good man and did good things.' "

INDEX OF PERSONS

Index

Index

Roosevelt, Mrs. Eleanor, 117
Russell, Bertram, 64, 66

Samuel, Mr. Herbert, 65
Sanders, Miss E. F., 26-7
Schnee, Dr. von, 111
Selassie, Haile, 109-10
Selbie, Dr. W. B., 75
Shepherd, Dr. Ambrose, 9, 12, 15, 32
Shillito, the Rev. George, 82
Simpson, Mrs., 110
Smith, Prof. George Adam, 35
Smuts, General, 56
Souter, Dr., 19
Southwell, Bishop of, 47
Spring-Rice, Sir Cecil, 69-70
Spurr, the Rev. F. C., 49
Steyn, President, 56

Tagore, Rabindranath, 23, 119
Taylor, W. T., 34
Thatcher, Principal (of Sydney), 19

Thomas, Margaret, Lady Rhondda, 27
Tocher, Dr. J. F., 34

Vanburgh, Irene and Violet, 27
Veitch, T. N., 93

Water, te, 109
Warren, Miss, 25
Watson, Mr. Walter, 13
Wet, General de, 56
Willoughby, Dr., 54
Wilson, the Rev. Dorothy, 91
Wilson, Major Frank (later General), 47
Wood, H. G., 80, 129
Wood, Willie, 13
Wyndham, the Rt. Hon. George, 16

Young, C. B., 19

Zetkin, Clara, 112

GEORGE ALLEN & UNWIN LTD
London: 40 Museum Street, W.C.1
Cape Town: 58–60 Long Street
Sydney, N.S.W.: 55 York Street
Toronto: 91 Wellington Street West
Calcutta: 17 Central Ave., P.O. Dharamtala
Bombay: 15 Graham Road, Ballard Estate
Wellington, N.Z.: 8 Kings Crescent, Lower Hutt